"When I began at Walt Disney Imagineering, almost everything about the business was conveyed through oral tradition. That was forty years ago. Margaret Kerrison has created a source with this book, *Immersive Storytelling*. The communal wisdom, experience, and real-world examples collected here represent a career's worth of exposure. Immerse yourself."

— Joe Rohde, Veteran Executive of Walt Disney Imagineering

"Margaret invites every writer or would-be writer to consider their world building from a 360 degree vantage point. She also dares to make it personal. Margaret's belief is that the personal, if handled correctly, can be universal, and is an invitation for all of us, regardless of ethnicity, nationality, or gender to investigate why the stories we want to tell matter."

— Shelby Jiggetts-Tivony, Vice President Creative & Advanced Development, Disney Live Entertainment

"Immersive storytelling in themed environments is an evolving, audience-driven, and play-focused medium that has lacked serious, practical, and conversational dissection. Until now. Throughout this book, Margaret Kerrison illustrates the artistry of so-called escapism, making the case that the entertainment we experience will continue to blur the lines between the storyteller and story participant. Entering a story is no mere escape; it's how we make sense of the world around us."

— Todd Martens, theme park journalist for the *Los Angeles Times*

"Margaret Kerrison's 'guide' is the first and most clearly laid out exploration of next gen storytelling that I've encountered. It serves both as an overview for the curious and a manual for the professional. It is in and of itself, a story well told."

— Danny Bilson, Chair, Interactive Media and Games Division, University of Southern California

"Margaret Kerrison's voice as a storyteller, as an expert, and as a woman of color is critically valuable to this industry. Her stories have been transformed into epic landscapes and deeply emotional experiences across galaxies, eras, and genres. And that world-building power is all right here at your fingertips. Use it well."

— Amber Samdahl, Former Executive Creative Director, Walt Disney Imagineering

"Peeking behind the curtain often zaps all the magic out of whatever's behind it. Excitingly, *Immersive Storytelling* offers a rare exception, where its insights, guidance, and wisdom combine to shine an even brighter light on the incredible sorcery underlying the world-building process."

— David Baronoff, Founder, Chief Cross-Media Officer, Bad Robot Games

"There is very little more important or more foundational to our lives than storytelling. Whether you are writing a screenplay, curating a museum, designing a theme park ride, or reinventing a retail experience — in fact, anyone curious about how to create the best possible immersive experience, you will find this book friendly, useful, and very interesting."

— Catherine Powell, Global Head of Hosting - Airbnb, Former President of the Disney Parks, Western Region

"Creating stories for location-based, interactive experiences comes with a completely unique set of challenges than other narrative fiction, and there is no better guide book to mastering this relatively new medium than Margaret Kerrison's amazing *Immersive Storytelling*. From theme to worldbuilding to breaking into the industry, this book has everything you need to become an expert interactive storyteller."

— Matt Martin, Sr. Creative Executive, Lucasfilm Story (

T0346732

"Driven by an approach to storytelling rooted in genuine curiosity, empathy, and a deep interest in what speaks to the hearts of audiences, Margaret's book invites readers on a journey of discovery. Through clear explanation, she illustrates the interdependence between story and design, demystifying our artform, from the biggest ideas down to the ever-critical details. I wish I had this book when I was just starting out, but I am delighted to have it now. Illuminating!"

> — Nancy Seruto, Creative Executive, Recipient of 2020 Buzz Price Lifetime Achievement Award

"Margaret Kerrison's brilliant book, *Immersive Storytelling*, at last gives us a definitive guide to story-making for location-based entertainment, backed by her real-world experience in story craftsmanship. No matter what field you are in, this book will help you create compelling stories that capture and hold the hearts and the attention of your audience."

> —Bob Rogers, Founder & CEO, BRC Imagination Arts

"Margaret Kerrison's *Immersive Storytelling* is written like an immersive experience. Her unique abilities and personal experience combined with a love of universal storytelling create a roadmap for the reader to find their space and comfort within this book."

> — Diana Williams, Award-winning Producer, Co-Founder of Kinetic Energy Entertainment

"Immersive storytelling is the art of the extraordinary, taking our minds to other places, to something new, exciting. Story is all around us and part of us. This book helps us better understand how to see and to map the process that makes story possible. It is a testament to that art and work of giving voice and form to stories that matter."

> — Zach Riddley, Creative Portfolio Executive, Walt Disney Imagineering

"For those of us who have forged long careers in the world of immersive storytelling, we have come to understand that our path is not a choice, but what we were put on this earth to do. *Immersive Storytelling* offers indispensable tools for all storytellers across disciplines. Whatever the problem you are faced with, no matter how challenging or in what industry, the bottom line to any solution is story. Identifying a compelling story and realizing it in a way that will touch the human spirit, never fails to provide the answer."

> — Valerie Faithorn, Principal, Storyspace Design, Inc.

"Regardless of whether one works to create memorable experiences drawn from history or fantasy, is a veteran storyteller or just beginning to explore story's power, Margaret has provided a wonderfully readable book that lays down a firm framework to actively enable us to build the kind of unique connections through stories that help us understand ourselves and each other."

> — Taylor Stoermer, Lecturer in Museum and Heritage Studies, Advanced Academic Programs, Johns Hopkins University

"I can think of no better guide through the world of immersive storytelling than Margaret Kerrison. This book is like having her as your personal mentor right by your side, dispensing her insights and drawing on her collected wisdom and experience in this industry. Whether you're looking to break into this exciting medium or even if you're a seasoned veteran, you will find much to inspire you here. Follow Margaret's lead and you will not regret it!"

> — Steven Spiegel, Story Editor Executive, Walt Disney Imagineering

"After attending a great immersive production, many people are inspired to try their hand at crafting one. The vast majority quickly find themselves at a loss as to where to even begin. Finally, Margaret Kerrison has given them an answer. Here. With this book. They start here."

> — Noah J. Nelson, Publisher of *No Proscenium*

IMMERSIVE STORY TELLING FOR REAL AND IMAGINED WORLDS

A Writer's Guide

MARGARET CHANDRA KERRISON

MICHAEL WIESE PRODUCTIONS

Published by Michael Wiese Productions
12400 Ventura Blvd. #1111
Studio City, CA 91604
(818) 379-8799, (818) 986-3408 (FAX)
mw@mwp.com
www.mwp.com

Cover design by Johnny Ink
Copyediting by Sarah Beach

Manufactured in the United States of America

Copyright © 2022 by Margaret Chandra Kerrison
First Printing 2022

All rights reserved. No part of this book may be reproduced in any form or by any means without permission in writing from the author, except for the inclusion of brief quotations in a review.

Library of Congress Cataloging-in-Publication Data

Names: Kerrison, Margaret Chandra, author.
Title: The immersive storyteller : writing for real and imagined worlds /
by Margaret Chandra Kerrison.
Description: Studio City, CA : Michael Wiese Productions, [2022] | Summary:
"How do you take an idea from inspiration to manifestation? How do you
move from telling a story to creating a world? In this richly
illustrated book, the first of its kind written specifically for
writers, Kerrison lays out the craft of immersive storytelling. She uses
case studies to show what works, and highlights the essential role of
the writer on a complex creative team. Ready to take the kernel of an
idea and turn it into a full-fledged experience? This book gives you the
blueprint"– Provided by publisher.
Identifiers: LCCN 2021047410 | ISBN 9781615933419 (trade paperback)
Subjects: LCSH: Authorship. | Storytelling.
Classification: LCC PN151 .K43 2022 | DDC 808.02–dc23/eng/20220302
LC record available at https://lccn.loc.gov/2021047410

CONTENTS

DEDICATION

To Foster and Bryce, the love and joy of my life.

FOREWORD
SCOTT TROWBRIDGE

I have been a ghost, a space-warrior, a time-traveler, a detective, and a refugee. I have traveled to the far reaches of the galaxy, stepped inside someone else's imagination, and saw "myself" through the critical eyes of a third-party observer.

Well, at least I have participated in carefully crafted experiences designed to help me *believe* that I have done those things. All that, and more, is possible through the artful creation of authored environments, events, and journeys that we collectively label *immersive experiences*. And even if the events were artificial simulations or fabrications, the experience, the discoveries, and the emotional responses were, and still are, decidedly real.

Everywhere you look today, you can find experiences designed to immerse yourself in an imagined reality, or to provide a specific encounter with an alternate perspective of reality. And as the experience economy continues to expand, there are more and more categories of immersive experience than ever before. Going well beyond theme parks and museums, immersive experience design is influencing restaurants, brand experiences, retail experiences, corporate visitor centers, escape rooms, sports venues, social media venues, airlines, site-specific music, and theatrical performances to name a few. And every day, this very incomplete list is growing.

Accelerating this growth are entirely new modes of technology-driven immersion that didn't exist just a few years ago; at home virtual-reality headsets, location based virtual-reality experiences, phone-based augmented or "mixed" reality experiences. All of these emerging, tech-driven media utilize many of the same principals, and rely on the same fundamental and universally human forms of interaction, relationship, and meaning that immersive experiences and stories characterize so well.

And if that wasn't enough, these core techniques, principles, and benefits of immersive experience design are increasingly relied upon outside of entertainment and education as well; from helping you navigate a complex city transit system to providing a narrative framework to help somebody process a stressful personal experience. The benefits derived from understanding and deliberately designing the way someone progresses through an experience, and the relationships and connections involved, are adding value in more unexpected, and important, venues. As an example, I think most people would be surprised at the amount of design and story thinking currently underway to improve the modern medical patient experience.

The primary driver at the heart of all of these experiences, or at least should be, is the concept of STORY. It is that thing we call *story* that gives the participants, the location, the events, and our relationship to all of these factors, a framework for relating, discovering, and understanding. When successful, it provides meaning and even personal transformation. Story has been at the heart of how we see ourselves and the world around us (whether real or imagined), from the first time a group gathered around a campfire to hear tales of the hunt, to the most modern, state of the art tech-driven immersive experience.

But what makes a story or an experience "immersive"? That's the million-dollar question. There are no set rules around it so the adage of "you know it when you see it" could be modified to "you know it when you're in it" and eventually to "you know it when you believe it." There might be one over-arching conceptual question one can use to distinguish between immersive and presentational experiences, and it is critical to the understanding of how to craft story and narrative for these experiences. That distinction is the point-of-view of the audience.

Is your audience's experiential context distinct from the characters or participants? Is the audience intentionally separated from them by some element like the rectangle of a cinema or television screen or a theatrical proscenium? Or is your experience mediated by artificially arranged seating or staging intended to differentiate audience from participant? Conversely, is the experience designed to have the audience and the other participants share the same contextual reality? It's the difference between being within or separate, a spectator or a participant. This might seem an overly intellectual question if all you are wanting to do is create a cool brand experience for a client, but understanding this framing choice and its incumbent pros and cons, is the first crucial step to crafting story and narrative for this strange, complex, always-doing-things-for-the-first-time, quirky, delightful and POWERFUL medium. If seeing is believing, then doing is understanding.

I have had the privilege of working alongside storytellers that have authored some of the most beloved stories of recent generations. And in doing so, I have seen the difference that is made when you put a strong, relatable story at the heart of an experience vs when that story, narrative, or thematic core is weak or missing. It is as true of any movie as it is of a theme park attraction or corporate visitor center. Story drives meaning. Story creates connection. Story allows us to transcend through the intellectual into the emotional. And from the specifics of accuracy into the bigger shared truths that reflect our humanity.

While the basics of story are universal no matter the medium, the specifics of crafting story for immersive experiences are quite quirky and challenging. They serve up a collection of unique opportunities:

- How to construct a frame for your story (every story has one).
- How to invite and connect with an audience.
- How to communicate expectations and establish the ground rules of participation.
- How to accommodate the inputs of participants in the narrative without breaking it.
- How to determine what is and isn't actually important in your story.
- And, not to be dismissed, how to get this all done in the context of a professional workplace and as part of a dynamic team.

The craft and profession of writing for this broad category of immersive experiences offers no shortage of challenges and discoveries, but also no shortage of fun.

I have had the privilege of working alongside Margaret for the last six years. I have seen firsthand just what it takes to meld the mechanics of narrative structure, the peculiar nuances of participatory experiences, and to shape it all into the service of meaningful and relevant overarching themes and goals. Many times, as we've sat around our own campfire, crafting the stories and experiences we want to tell, we have come to rely on some of the tips, tricks, exercises, and insights that Margaret has collected in this book — of course, it was usually a messy conference room and not a campfire.

There is no guaranteed method to creating great stories. Every project has its own collection of unique opportunities, constraints, audience, and intent. However, the ideas contained in this book can hopefully convey some version of the alchemy of wisdom, inspiration, experience, and perseverance that Margaret has provided to every project that we've worked on together. This book can provide a valuable service to the prospective professional by outlining just what the expectations, deliverables, working dynamics, and rewards are for those who choose to craft immersive stories and experiences as a profession.

I firmly believe that a story well-told can change the world. I believe that a story well-lived through immersive experience can motivate and personalize transformational change. I've been working to make that true for most of my professional life, and I've been lucky enough to do that in the company of so many amazing colleagues. And while I realize that I'm lucky enough to have Margaret return my texts when I bother her at midnight, I hope that this book and the ideas, insights, and prompts it offers, can provide some of that same benefit for you. And, if that doesn't work, just do what I do. Text Margaret. 24/7. Her number is "(xxx) xxx-xxxx."

INTRODUCTION

From the time I learned how to read and write, I loved to tell stories. First, it came in the form of journaling in first grade, then writing short stories, then drawing my own comic books, making my own puppets and boardgames, videorecording my own skits, taping my own radio show, designing costumes, drawing elaborate plans for my future home, and writing fantastical poems and macabre plays. I was that kid who was doodling or writing when I should've paid more attention in science or math class. I absolutely had to create. It was something that came naturally to me and it was a pastime I enjoyed.

Over the past fourteen years, I've written stories and consulted for independent artists, theme parks, museums, children's animated shows, independent feature films, TV shows, documentaries, small design agencies, and *Fortune* 500 companies. My most recent projects at Walt Disney Imagineering include *Star Wars: Galaxy's Edge, Star Wars: Galactic Starcruiser, Avengers Campus, Guardians of the Galaxy: Cosmic Rewind,* and National Geographic HQ.

I discovered the world of immersive storytelling when I was working towards a graduate screenwriting degree at the University of Southern California School of Cinematic Arts. I was in my thesis class working on a feature film script inspired by the story of the only female emperor of China, named Wu Zetian. It was a few months before graduation and I was experiencing a looming anxiety to find a job in the entertainment industry.

Our professor, Pam Douglas, motivated us to find work in other industries besides film and television. She started to list examples of all the writing jobs we can pursue in other industries, such as gaming, animation, and theme parks. I remember thinking, they need writers to write stories for theme parks? Who does that? That sounds awesome. I've always been a fan of theme parks, but I never thought a writer could ever have a career in it. My curiosity was piqued.

That evening at home, I searched for "designing theme parks" and found the exciting world of immersive storytelling. I found a website for a group called Themed Entertainment Association, an "international non-profit association representing the world's leading creators, developers, designers and producers of compelling places and experiences."[1]

One day when I was visiting the Norton Simon Museum in Pasadena, California, I found myself wandering around the South and Southeast Asian Paintings and Sculpture collection. It was an intimate, serene, and thoughtfully-designed space that reminded me of home. I wondered who designed this beautiful space. I sat down on a bench and looked out at the garden behind the window, where a large granite Buddha statue sat across from me.

Surely, someone or a group of people were responsible for designing this experience and deciding what went where and why. They must have also considered how the visitor walked through the space and what objects they would encounter first before turning the corner and discovering

[1] https://www.teaconnect.org/index.cfm

a new object. That notion excited me. Could there be a storyteller that helped to define and design these spaces? How did they do it?

After visiting the museum, I went back to the TEA website and found a wealth of information, news, mentoring, networking, and job opportunities. One of the links provided a Member Directory, which I promptly clicked. I searched for companies located in California and started emailing the companies that I found interesting. In the e-mail, I introduced myself as a student who was finishing my graduate degree in screenwriting from USC, and provided my internship and freelance work experiences while I was a student.

Many months later, I finally received a reply to one of my query emails, from a company called BRC Imagination Arts based in Burbank, California. They asked to meet with me based on my writing samples. Even though I didn't have any experience working for an experience design company, they took a chance on me.

I started working with them promptly after I wrapped up with a freelance TV gig, and worked on a project called the Heineken Experience, a historic brewery attraction and corporate visitor center for the internationally distributed Dutch pilsner, Heineken. I loved everything about the work and enjoyed collaborating with multiple disciplines in the same team, but most importantly, I was paid to be a writer. It was inspiring to work with nice, passionate, and talented people who were so committed to creating experiences based on a strong story foundation.

BRC kept me on for many projects after the Heineken Experience. I will be forever grateful to them and to their founder, Bob Rogers, for taking me under their wing and shaping me into the writer and creator that I am today. With BRC, I worked on many other projects, including the Louisiana Old State Capitol (Baton Rouge, Louisiana), NASA Kennedy Space Center Visitor Complex (Cape Canaveral, Florida), AMOREPACIFIC Story Garden (Osan, South Korea), and the Information and Communications Pavilion for the Shanghai World Expo 2010 (Shanghai, China). I was a writer on three projects that earned Thea Awards during my four years working at BRC.

I was a freelance consultant for four more years, working with a variety of companies until I noticed a job posting from Walt Disney Imagineering for a Show Writer position. I knew I had to get my foot in the door, and sent messages on LinkedIn to the hiring manager of the story department at the time, and found a couple of Imagineers in my network to put in a good word for me. I knew that I had to do everything in my power to get that job. I got glowing recommendation letters from my previous employers, worked hard to revise my best writing samples, and rehearsed my interviews. After many months of emails and phone calls, waiting, and a few rounds of interviews, I was devastated to find out that I didn't get the position.

I tried to move on with my life, and continued to work on other freelance projects. It hurt that I was so close to my dream that I could touch it, but I wasn't "good enough" to make the cut. Even with the disappointing news, I didn't give up. I continued to email and keep in touch with the hiring manager. It pays to be persistent.

Many months later, the hiring manager set up a meeting for me to chat with the Executive Producer and the Executive Creative Director regarding a freelance consultant gig as the land writer for a confidential project. That secret project turned out to be the "*Star Wars* project." When one door closes, another one opens.

That was seven years ago. Little did I know that one day I would be the overall story lead for one of the most ambitious lands ever built by Walt Disney Imagineering. I feel like the last seven years at Imagineering have been a masterclass in designing immersive spaces and experiences. Not only have I met some of the most talented people I've ever met in my life, everyone from graphic designers to audio engineers, I've also discovered this burning desire to continually improve and perfect my craft. Being around so many talented people made me want to be better. I was inspired by their work ethic, their passion and enthusiasm, and their unwavering spirit in some of the most challenging times. These Imagineers led by example and showed me what it meant to be the best in class for creating memorable experiences for the whole family.

I wondered what it would be like to write a book for aspiring writers in this industry. There's so much to share, and I want to pass on my learnings and insights to the next generation of storytellers. As a fan of experiences, I'm curious to see where this medium of storytelling leads, and hope to impart some helpful tips and tools that will take this medium to the next level.

When I was in the early stages of writing this book, I was reminded of the many e-mails and LinkedIn messages from aspiring writers and creatives looking to break into the industry. They were asking for my advice and were curious to know what I did in my job. They also asked how I do what I do, especially after seeing me (with many other talented Imagineers I'm fortunate enough to call my friends) appear in our free online course *Imagineering in a Box,* a wonderful series we developed in collaboration with Kahn Academy and the Pixar in a Box team.

IMAGINEERING IN A BOX

If you've never heard of this free online series before, check it out! *Imagineering in a Box* is designed to pull back the curtain to show you how writers, artists, designers and engineers work together to create theme parks and other immersive experiences. Go behind the scenes with Disney Imagineers and complete project-based exercises to design a theme park of your very own. It's perfect for middle and high school students looking to design their own project in a lesson-by-lesson program that includes video content as well as multidisciplinary exercises.

I was getting e-mails from middle school kids who wanted nothing more than to be an Imagineer one day. They were girls who loved science and engineering, boys who loved to build things out of LEGO bricks, and adults who never stopped dreaming. They wanted to pick my brain and chat with me about my career.

For all those people who reached out to me and for those who thought about reaching out to me but never did, I'm writing this book for you. Hopefully, I can impart some wisdom from my experiences working in this exciting industry.

The first tip: there are no hard and fast rules. This is not a textbook nor is it a "how to" book. I would regard this book as a "guide" of helpful tips and tools. Each individual and company approaches their processes and projects differently. I will share my collected wisdom and best practices, which will hopefully help you find your own approach.

Seek out mentors, find opportunities that interest you, and be persistent in going for what you want. It's important to create a daily habit to improve your craft and constantly learn from others. You should never stop writing (even when you have bad writing days), and you should never stop learning (even when you're on projects that you're not as excited about). With more experience, you'll have the confidence to "break the rules" so that you can create something truly unique and innovative. Ultimately, you want to find a style and method that is most appealing to you.

This is a very rewarding industry to work in as a writer. Those of us who are fortunate enough to work as writers in creating experiences that connect people often feel like that this isn't "work." We are given an incredible opportunity to create stories and spaces for people to play together. As storytellers, we strive to create experiences that are moving, compelling, and meaningful. We design spaces so that visitors can escape and leave their ordinary lives behind. We make places where the audience can see

themselves and feel a sense of connection and belonging. We make experiences full of magic so that we are
reminded that our lives are magical in themselves.

As a creator, storyteller, and writer, there is nothing more
satisfying than to see audiences engage and immerse
themselves in stories I helped to shape. To know that I
bring magic into people's lives is the greatest reward I
can hope for. To see families, friends, and couples create
memories in experiences that I helped to create is in one
word – everything.

I hope that you find some tidbits and inspiration in this
book to create your stories so that I may have the privilege
of experiencing them one day. I look forward to seeing
what the future generations create in the world of immersive storytelling. Please be sure to invite me!

Margaret Kerrison

THIS IS *NOT* A TEXTBOOK

Regard this book as a guide of collected wisdom, insights, and impressions, rather than a prescriptive "how to write for immersive storytelling" book. This medium of storytelling requires you to think differently. Unlike writing a feature or TV script, where there are certain formats and story structures to adhere to, the beauty of this medium is that there's room for flexibility, creativity, and innovation. The moment that you believe that creating an immersive experience is like following a recipe, you're doomed.

Rather than give you the answers, I'll help you to ask the right questions. Often times, immersive storytellers and designers jump into a project without spending the necessary time to ask the most important questions of storytelling. I'll guide you through a series of questions and prompts that will open your mind to thinking about your experience differently.

Push the boundaries, change the rules, and think outside the box. Think differently, but familiarize yourself with certain guidelines and best practices that I will share with you throughout the book. Often, I will use examples of successful storytelling in experiences today, to show you the breadth and depth of immersive storytelling around the world.

This is by no means a comprehensive encyclopedia of the best immersive experiences either. Don't be disheartened if you don't see your favorite attraction or experience included in this book. You may also completely disagree about the experiences I've chosen to highlight. The point is that immersive storytelling isn't any one thing. I want to share the experiences that have made an impression on me, to highlight some of the points I'm making.

You may read this book from cover-to-cover. You may pick it up from time to time to read particular sections that may be handy when you need inspiration. You may just read for the sake of learning something new. My hope is that you will find some tips, insights, and wisdom that can inspire you to change the world, one immersive experience at a time.

These are the different groups of people who might find this book useful.

ASPIRING WRITERS & DESIGNERS

You're looking to get into the wonderful world of immersive storytelling and don't know where to start. You love to write and you want to get paid to write creatively, but you don't know anyone in the industry. This book is meant to give you a crash course in writing and developing stories for experiences, so that you may start knocking on some of those doors. Whether it be in writing for museums, theme parks, immersive environments, rides, shows, or other forms of immersive storytelling like video games and AR/VR, you may find this book useful in your writing process. I hope that I can give you some tips and starter thoughts to begin your journey in writing for this rewarding industry.

JUMPSTART SEEKERS

You may be in need of inspiration. You may be lost as to how to start your project or perhaps you're stuck in the middle of your project and have lost your way. I hope that the questions I pose for you and the examples of storytelling I provide will be a jumpstart to your creative engine. We all get lost sometimes. It's a perfectly natural process in creative writing. I haven't met one single talented individual who doesn't get into a slump every so often when it comes to writing or telling their stories. It's a very good indicator that you are an artist who takes pride in your work.

CURIOUS LEARNERS

You may just be curious about how we tell stories and write for immersive storytelling. The art of writing for this field is not always a linear narrative, so how do we even begin to tell our stories when we don't always have a clear beginning, middle, and end? How do you tell a story for a ride like a roller coaster? Does a food cart need a story? Why does a museum exhibit need an overarching theme and story? These are all questions writers should ask when developing a story for any experience. I'll also write about how we strive to make change in our viewers and visitors. Hint: It goes back to the age-old question of why we tell stories in the first place.

ADULTS WHO NEVER GREW UP

If you're that adult who likes to pretend that they're someone else for a while, play so hard with your kids that you tire them out, constantly daydream about being in another world, write stories in your head, imagine "what if" scenarios while standing in line with your groceries, work on cool projects in your backyard, put on plays for your friends, and make finger puppets out of felt just for the heck of it, then this book is for you. Maybe you should consider going into the immersive entertainment business — a world where you'll meet like-minded adults who never lost their sense of curiosity or childlike perspective of the world.

FOR ALL DREAMERS

No matter who you are, I hope that you find some inspiration and a reminder that you are creative and that *you can do it.* Don't let anyone tell you that this dream is impossible; that you should get a "regular job" that pays instead of pinning your hopes on a dream that you'll never get. Don't listen to the naysayers. Listen to your own voice. What does it tell you? If you believe this is the career for you, then go for it! Use every ounce of your strength and will to achieve it.

What people don't tell you is that your success isn't based on whether you're the most talented and brilliant writer in the room. It's really about being gracious, persistent, hardworking, and passionate. You have to make sure you want it. Like really, really want it.

A GREAT OPENING SCENE

HAUNTED MANSION
WRITTEN BY FRANCIS XAVIER ATENCIO

Guests enter the foyer and a SPOOKY ORGAN
plays. The doors shut.

> GHOST HOST
> (voice only)
> When hinges creak in doorless
> chambers and strange and frightening
> sounds echo through the halls;
> whenever candle lights flicker;
> where the air is deathly still --
> that is the time when ghosts are
> present, practicing their terror
> with ghoulish delight.

Doors open to a round room with portraits on
the walls. Guests enter.

> ATTENDANT
> Step directly toward the dead center
> of the gallery, please.

> GHOST HOST
> (voice only)
> Welcome foolish mortals to the
> **Haunted Mansion.** I am your host --
> your <u>ghost</u> host. Kindly step all
> the way in please and make room for
> everyone. There's no turning back
> now...

> Our tour begins here in this
> gallery, where you see paintings of

some of our guests as they appeared
in their corruptible mortal state.

The doors shut.

> GHOST HOST
> (voice only)
> Your cadaverous pallor betrays
> an aura of foreboding, almost as
> though you sense a disquieting
> metamorphosis. Is this haunted
> room actually stretching? Or is it
> your imagination? And consider this
> dismaying observation: this chamber
> has no windows and no doors. Which
> offers you this chilling challenge:
> to find a way out.

> GHOST HOST
> (voice only; laughs)
> Of course, there's always my way!

The lights go out. There is a LOUD SCREAM.

Guests leave the gallery and enter a hallway
filled with portraits. The SOUND of THUNDER
shakes the room.

> GHOST HOST
> (voice only)
> Oh, I didn't mean to frighten you
> prematurely. The real chills come
> later. Now, as they say, "look
> alive" and we'll continue our little
> tour. And let's all stay together,
> please.
>
> There are several prominent ghosts
> who have retired here from creepy
> old crypts all over the world.
> Actually, we have nine hundred and
> ninety-nine happy haunts here. But
> there's room for a thousand. Any
> volunteers?

(laughter)
If you insist on lagging behind, you
may not need to volunteer.

Guests approach the boarding area.

GHOST HOST
(voice only)
And now, a carriage approaches to
take you into the boundless realm
of the supernatural. Take your loved
ones by the hand please, and kindly
watch your step. Oh yes. And no
flash pictures please. We spirits
are frightfully sensitive to bright
lights.

Guests board a "doom buggy," which travels
upwards toward a grand staircase.

GHOST HOST
(voice only)
Do not pull down on the safety bar,
please. I will lower it for you.
And heed this warning: the spirits
will materialize only if you remain
quietly seated at all times.

We find it delightfully unlivable
here in this ghostly retreat. Every
room has wall-to-wall creeps and
hot and cold running chills. Hmm...
Listen.

Guests pass an endless hallway where candles
float mid-air. There is a GHOSTLY MOANING.

One of the best opening scenes in the history of theme
park attractions, the Haunted Mansion is a classic. I experienced this ride in Tokyo Disneyland and it was *the* ride
that made me fall in love with theme parks. Like a good
TV script or feature screenplay, the first page is chockfull

of information. It sets up the world, characters, tone, mood, conflict, and genre. The scene is dramatic, suspenseful, creepy, and playful.

The first paragraph sets up the mood (dark, mysterious), tone (creepy, but playful), setting (a haunted place), and genre (spooky dark ride). The second paragraph introduces the visitors as "foolish mortals" and the disembodied voice as the "ghost host." Visitors get a sense that they belong in this world, as welcomed by the ghost host.

By the end of the first page, the visitor is given the conflict, which in this case, also serves as the "call to action" (an instruction to the hero/audience to make an immediate and desired action). "Find a way out" he tells the foolish mortals.

WHAT IS THE "CALL TO ACTION?"

In feature screenwriting, Act One of a script (approximately the first 30 pages of the script), establishes the status quo ("normal life" of the protagonist), the inciting incident (the event or character that disrupts the protagonist's status quo), and the call to adventure/action (the decision the protagonist makes in response to the inciting incident) that propels the protagonist (hero) into Act Two of the story.

To learn more about writing dramatic structure and narrative arcs (the overall shape of rising and falling tension or emotion in a story as first documented by Aristotle's *Poetics*), I've included a recommended reading list for all aspiring writers at the end of this book.

In the second page, visitors are given safety instructions (or "ride safety spiels" as we call them at Walt Disney Imagineering) for riding the "doom buggy" vehicle, but they are cleverly written to fit into the story and the setting. The ghost host also introduces the visitor to other characters in the story, the 999 "happy haunts" that live in the mansion. Finally, he invites the visitor to be the 1,000[th] happy haunt.

SCREENWRITING IS ONLY ONE PART OF THE JOB

Writing for this industry is more than just writing screenplays. In fact, the majority of your work is not screenwriting, but in helping your teams develop the stories of your experience. In later chapters, we'll delve into the various responsibilities and deliverables as the Story Lead/Writer, which include everything from shaping the overall story of your experience to writing copy for graphics and marketing materials.

In the gaming industry, there are roles for the Narrative Director, Narrative Designer, and Writer. The Narrative Director is responsible for the overall narrative of the game and manages the work of the Narrative Designers and Writers. Narrative Designers are responsible for the narrative of the player. Writers are responsible for the narrative of the characters in the game.

In the immersive entertainment industry, often times, the Story Lead/Writer has to do the work of the Narrative Director, Narrative Designer, and Writer. Of course, the scope of your work depends on the scale of the project. You may be able to hire other writers to help with the workload, but ultimately, you have to be a real Swiss army knife of a writer to succeed in this industry. You have to learn to be flexible, a quick study, open to feedback, and be a relentless story champion across multiple disciplines.

IMMERSING THE GUEST

"I don't want the public to see the world they live in while they're in the Park. I want them to feel they're in another world."

— *Walt Disney*[2]

Walt Disney was a master storyteller, and understood that he had to place his guests (a term he used to refer to his park visitors and is still used until today) in the story world if he wanted them to be engaged and emotionally-invested.

WALT DISNEY'S TERMS

Cast Members — The term referring to employees of Walt Disney Imagineering and Disney Parks, Resorts, and Cruise Lines. The origin of the term comes from Walt Disney's use of theatrical terms when referring to park operations.

Guests — The term referring to visitors of Disney Parks, Resorts, and Cruise Lines. An effective way to remind cast members that they are gracious hosts to their visitors.

Like a great filmmaker, he also understood that the opening scene is what grabs the attention of the guest, makes them feel present in the moment, and allows the guest to "suspend their disbelief."

---

[2] https://d23.com/walt-disney-quote/i-dont-want/

"Suspension of disbelief" is a concept that describes how, in order to become emotionally involved in a narrative, audiences must react as if the characters are real and the situation/events they find themselves in are happening now, even though they know it is only a fictional story. The willing suspension of disbelief for the moment was how the British poet Samuel Taylor Coleridge phrased it in 1817, with reference to the audiences for literary works.[3]

As a storyteller, Walt understood that he had to acknowledge the role of the audience and "invite them to play." Using his masterful storytelling skills, he designed Disneyland to draw out his guests' emotions based on their wish fulfillment and their willingness to suspend their disbelief.

---

[3] https://www.oxfordreference.com/view/10.1093/oi/authority.20110803100544310

WHAT IS IMMERSIVE STORYTELLING?

Immersive storytelling describes creating a space using different kinds of technology to build a sense of presence for the visitor/audience. The space can be a combination of physical, digital, and/or virtual elements, and ultimately, it gives the visitor a transportive feeling within an emotionally-compelling story as if they "are really there." An immersive space is designed to be so compelling that it makes visitors feel like they're part of that world and hopefully, make them believe that they belong in it. It's an impactful technique that captures the emotion and wish fulfillment of that experience.

Immersive storytelling can also be referred to as experience design, themed experience, immersive experience, and in its most extreme form — worldbuilding. The story can take place in many physical and digital environments: a theme park, museum, house, small exhibit, corporate center, restaurant, store, online learning site, virtual reality experience, game, or other forms.

Immersive stories can be original, or adapted from a different format, such as a book, toy, video game, film, theme park ride, or television series. They can be cultural and educational, like what you would experience in a national park exhibit, historical foundation, art museum, or science center. They can be inviting and customer-bonding, like what you would see in a pop-up event to introduce a new brand.

Immersive experiences can be small and intimate, like the Thea-award winning, *The Nest*, created by two former Imagineers, Jeff Leinenveber & Jarrett Lantz. On their website, they describe the show as

> an intimate, live experience for two audience members at a time, combining elements of immersive theater, narrative video games, serialized podcasts, and escape rooms into a new way to experience a story. Equipped with a flashlight, search through personal effects, explore your surroundings, and listen to audio cassettes to piece together the dramatic narrative of Josie's life.[4]

I experienced this little gem and loved the deceptively simple setup, yet every single detail of the story is meticulously designed to immerse visitors in this woman's life.

The Nest. Photo: Jeremey Connors courtesy of Scout Expedition Co.

---

[4] http://www.thenestshow.com

Immersive experiences may not necessarily follow a clear plot or storyline. They can be emotional and visceral, like *Rain Room*[5] by Hannes Koch and Florian Ortkrass, of the London-based art collective Random International, an immersive light and sound installation that is featured in multiple locations around the world, that simulates a storm and invites visitors to "control the weather" without getting wet.

Random International's *Rain Room* at Jackalope Pavilion Melbourne. Photo: Jolly Yau on Unsplash.

---

[5] https://www.jackalopehotels.com/art/rainroom

They can be fun and whimsical, like Yayoi Kusama's mirror-based art installation *Infinity Mirrored Room — The Souls of Millions of Light Years Away* (2013)[6] or her art installation titled *with all my love for the tulips, I pray forever* (2011),[7] a room completely covered in huge polka dots.

One of my personal favorites, Korean artist Do Ho Suh's magnificent life-sized fabric sculptures of building interiors, like *348 West 22nd Street* (2011–15),[8] allows visitors to walk through a full-scale, ephemeral representation of the artist's former apartment in the Chelsea neighborhood of New York City.

They can be playful, immersive, and interactive, like the various teamLab art installations found around the world, which encourage visitors to explore, wander, discover, and interact with works of art that respond to touch and movement.

Immersive experiences can simply be fun, like a virtual reality experience or escape room found in places like Two Bit Circus, an "interactive digital playground of amusement for all ages"[9] where you can work together to blast aliens, ride on a roller coaster, or defend your raft from supernatural creatures.

---

[6] https://www.thebroad.org/art/yayoi-kusama
[7] https://www.worldartfoundations.com/marciano-art-foundation-yayoi-kusama-love-tulips-pray-forever-2011/
[8] https://www.lacma.org/art/exhibition/do-ho-suh-348-west-22nd-street
[9] https://twobitcircus.com

My son going on a virtual roller coaster ride in Two Bit Circus. Photo: Margaret Kerrison

They can take form in varying scales, from small intimate rooms to expansive multi-acre lands. The most extreme form of themed experiences will engage all of your senses — sight, sound, taste, touch, and smell. The most compelling experiences inspire a change in you.

YOU ARE THE STORY CHAMPION

Writing for immersive storytelling requires you to be the story champion and subject matter expert for the story of the experience. Does that mean that if you're working on an historical exhibit, you have to know everything a historian does? Not quite, but you do have to understand and appreciate the content, so that you can draw out the most compelling stories that will engage your audience. Like the writer of a good book or film, you have to appreciate what makes a story compelling to someone who doesn't know anything about the subject. You have to find the why of the experience; the deeper meaning and importance of the story.

THE S.T.O.R.Y. METHOD – THE FIRST FIVE QUESTIONS

At the start of every project, I always ask myself five questions. This is my personal method, in which I start to think about the most important elements of story. I use the word "story" as an acronym to remind me of the questions.

S — Share: Why share this story with the world?

If you, as the storyteller, don't know why you're sharing this story with the world, then no one will care about your story. Finding the why of the story is the most important question to ask. Storytelling is universal when you are honest. Honesty always finds the truth. With truth, comes the opportunity to open your audience's minds.

T — Theme: What's the theme of the experience?
Like any good story, your experience needs a theme. Once you understand why you're sharing this story with

the world, then you can develop the theme, or meaning, of the experience. The theme drives the narrative thrust of your experience. The narrative thrust is the building of main story beats (identifiable moments of change) that move your story forward in a dramatic way.

O — One-of-a-Kind: How can I make this experience unique?

I consider the many ways I can make the experience something that isn't already out there. The competition for your visitor's attention is immense. You want to ensure that your experience is memorable and one-of-a-kind; something that will quickly capture the imagination of the visitor.

R — Reflect: Why am I the best person to tell this story?

This is a big one. Why? Because knowing who you are as a storyteller will help give your experience a perspective. I've been asked to work on various projects based in Southeast Asia because I spent my childhood there. However, I've also had to work on many topics that I knew very little about. Finding your unique perspective is key to developing a compelling story.

Y — Yearn: What will visitors yearn to experience? What is their wish fulfillment?

Last but not least, questioning your visitor's greatest fantasy is something you must always consider. In order to do that, you have to understand what they are longing for. Is it belonging, connection, love, adventure, escape, transformation? Is it a chance for them to follow in the footsteps of their heroes? Is it to become heroes themselves?

If I can't answer these five questions, then I'm in trouble. If I, as the writer and storyteller, don't know why I'm sharing the story with the world, what's the theme, what makes it unique, why I'm the best storyteller for it, and what the audience yearns, then the project will struggle.

There will be many times in your career that you'll find yourself working on a subject, intellectual property, or brand that you're not very excited about. The most important thing is to find *your* connection to the story. You have to become a fan in order to reach the fans, which brings me to this very important fact:

**Find a little bit of yourself in the story,
and your audience will find a little bit of the story in
themselves**.

Find what makes you excited about the subject and it will most likely be the reason that others will be drawn to that subject. Talk to other people who have great passion for the subject, so you can develop a deeper understanding and connection to it. We are all unique in our perspectives, approaches, and storytelling abilities. Find your connection to the subject, and you'll have an easier time developing your unique perspective and approach in sharing the story with your audience.

Ultimately, if you, as the story champion, don't care about the experience, then why should your audience? Once you have found your unique connection and have fully committed to the project, then you give it everything you've got. If your heart and mind are behind the project every step of the way, there's no stopping you. Reach for the stars and DREAM BIG.

"Storytellers" plaque at Disney California Adventure Park. Photo: Margaret Kerrison

THE CREATIVE PROCESS

"The first step is to research. Read the books, watch the
media, listen to the scholars. You need to listen first.
Then you can build empathy."

— *Nancy Seruto*

RESEARCH

Before you start any project, the first step is to research
and educate yourself on your project's subject matter. It's
important that you take a scholarly approach to it, so that
you may talk intelligently about the topic with others.
Learning the vocabulary and gathering all the relevant
information jumpstarts your journey to building empathy
and appreciation for your subject matter. Educating yourself on the subject also demonstrates that you are giving
the topic the respect and dedication that it deserves.

The process for creating a real world versus an imagined
world is quite different. As I learned from Nancy Seruto,
award-winning producer, design consultant, and former
Creative Executive at Walt Disney Imagineering, the process for the museum exhibition industry (real world)
starts with understanding the details before building up
to the Big Idea.

REAL WORLD DESIGN PROCESS

Details

↓

Big Idea

In the process of designing a *real world* experience, you have to understand the facts from varying points-of-view. Gone are the days of authoring a story from one person's perspective. You have to bring in the experts and scholars and learn as much as possible about the details of a subject before attempting to shape the narrative. In the research process, you collect all of the significant and relevant details that begin to shape your Big Idea.

The process for creating an *imagined world*, however, is the reverse. You begin with the Big Idea and then you build the details.

IMAGINED WORLD DESIGN PROCESS

Big Idea

↓

Details

In creating an imagined world, you start with the Big Idea. You want to visit a *Star Wars* planet. You want to visit the world of *Harry Potter*. You want to step into a dream world. You want to become a spy. Once you've established the Big Idea, then you develop the details. What does it mean to visit a *Star Wars* planet? Which planet do you choose?

What's the significance of this planet? What will visitors do there? Who will they meet?

For your visitors, a *real world* experience builds their understanding of a topic before they walk away with a new appreciation, understanding, and empathy for a topic. In an *imagined world* experience, your visitors begin their journey based on the promise of the experience and discover all the wonderful details it has to offer. In both worlds, your visitor should ultimately walk away, transformed.

BRAINSTORMING

After the research period, a project kicks off with a brainstorming session, otherwise known in the industry as a design "charrette." It's a multi-disciplinary work session that runs for one or more days and involves all the key team members including, but not limited to, the producer, creative director, writer, artist, designer, and others. Traditionally, a design charrette serves as an intense period of design for a group of designers to draft a solution to a design problem. This period of time is also when the team develops the Big Idea. The Big Idea is the intent and mission of the project and answers the big questions of the experience. There may be mood boards (images of the subject matter, the location of the experience, the characters, and whatever else is relevant to the project) hung around the room to spark ideas and promote discussion.

Often times, there's one person who runs the charrette, either a creative director, or creative producer, and they guide the team in mapping out the experience by asking questions and leading ideation sessions. Charrettes are collaborative and interactive. They start with the under-standing that there's "no stupid idea." The point of the charrette is to capture *all* of the ideas, big and small.

THE BIG IDEA

How do you formulate your Big Idea? It's important that the charrette leader starts with the big questions. I start by asking my big five S.T.O.R.Y. questions: Why share this story with the world? What's the theme (or possible themes) of this experience? How can we make this experience unique? Why are we the best people to share this story? What is the visitor's wish fulfillment?

There are many other questions to consider: Where will they go? Who will they meet? What will they see? What are the "must-do" activities and experiences for our visitors? What do we want our visitors to feel? What are the big "wow" moments (the "Instagrammable" moments)? What's their emotional takeaway? How do we have them talking about this experience long after they leave? How do we stay connected with them?

These ideas are captured on index cards pinned to a board, or on large pieces of paper hung around the room. Team members can write ideas and walk over to the areas that they have ideas for, or the charrette leader can post them up for everyone to see and discuss. Artists can start drawing some rough sketches for their ideas and pin them up along with the written ideas.

Photo: Margaret Kerrison

After some ideas are shared, we typically see a pattern of themes and ideas. The leader can start separating some of the ideas into individual spaces/rooms for the visitors to experience. We start thinking about the visitor experience and flow. What do they see when they first walk in? Where do they go next? And where will they go after that?

An artist or the creative director will start to draw a bubble diagram on the board, large piece of paper, or write/ draw from their computer, to roughly capture the ideas and start developing the visitor flow of the experience.

WHAT'S A VISITOR FLOW?

A visitor flow describes the volume and movement of visitors to, and within, the buildings and spaces around and between them. The visitor flow considers how many visitors can be contained in the entire experience, in each individual space, what direction the visitors are moving towards, and the patterns of their movements. Understanding and maintaining a good visitor flow will provide an optimal experience for the visitor; one with fewer wait times, less crowding, and easier wayfinding, among other factors.

Each bubble is rough in concept and captures the scale of the space relative to the other spaces. The bigger bubbles show that these spaces will be larger compared to the smaller ones. It's a quick and fundamental way to capture the identity of the space without delving too deeply into the details. These spaces may change and iterate during the course of the project, but for the purposes of the charrette, it's a way for the team to visualize and prioritize the stories and spaces in the experience.

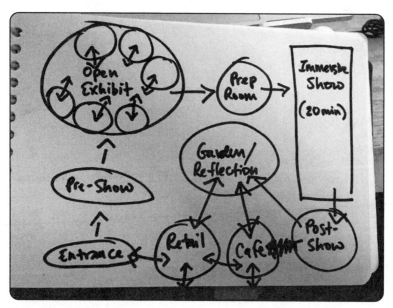

Photo: Margaret Kerrison

Depending on whether the flow of the visitor experience is linear or non-linear, it can be captured in different ways. You can use arrows to show the visitor flow if it's a more linear experience (e.g. virtual reality, escape rooms, rides, attractions, and other timed experiences), or your experience may be more open-ended in terms of how the visitor will explore the spaces. Ultimately, the bubble diagram shows all of the spaces/rooms that the visitors can discover and how they are connected to one another.

Here's an example of bubble headings for a linear experience:

1) Welcome/Lobby

2) Pre-show

3) Main show

4) Post-show

5) Retail

6) Exit

7) Café/Dining

8) Restrooms

9) Outdoor space

10) Parking

Here's an example of bubble headings for a non-linear experience (typical of museums and art galleries). Each room can be defined by different categories. This is typical in museums where objects are grouped by the objects' origin (country, region, etc.), artist, time period, format (photography, etc.) theme or story, or by the objects themselves (masks, ceramics, etc.).

1) Welcome/Lobby

2) First room/gallery

3) Second room/gallery

4) Third room/gallery

5) Fourth room/gallery

6) Retail

7) Exit

8) Café/Dining

9) Restrooms

10) Outdoor space

11) Parking

As you develop the identity for each bubble/space, it's important to remind yourself to tell one story at a time. Each of the bubbles warrants its own subplot or storyline, which supports the greater theme and story of the experience. You don't have to delve too deeply into each space just yet, but consider why each space is necessary to support the story foundation of the experience.

TELL ONE STORY AT A TIME

Telling one story at a time is not a new concept, but one that was clearly highlighted as one of *Mickey's Ten Commandments* by Disney Legend Marty Sklar. Consider the purpose of a logline for a movie or television series. In just one sentence, you should be able to describe your story succinctly. In film school, we learned that screenwriters reveal one new piece of information per scene. Put all the scenes together and you have a movie. The same goes with designing themed experiences. Tell one story/

establish one goal for each scene and you have an experience that feels emotionally engaging. Don't overthink it. Keep it simple so that even a five-year old kid understands what's going on.

Haunted Mansion Holiday in Disneyland, Photo: Margaret Kerrison

Determining the story for each scene requires the storyteller to first understand the emotion of the experience. It's no surprise that when the creators developed the Haunted Mansion in Disneyland, they wanted the audience to feel scared. But how do you scare the audience without merely doing jump-scares and loud sound effects? The team did their research and were inspired by real stories, such as the creepy story of Sarah Winchester from the Winchester Mystery House in San Jose, California. They also made up their own stories, such as a tale of a ghostly sea captain who killed his bride.

The question, then, was which scary stories did they want to tell and how did they all relate to the Haunted Mansion? They came up with the brilliant idea of creating a "Ghost Host" character who challenged visitors to find a way out … or join the other ghosts as their 1,000th "happy haunt." As they iterated their idea, Walt and his team added humor into the attraction, so that it could be fun for all ages.

Walt knew early on that he wanted his "guests" (how Walt referred to the park visitors) to feel like they were part of the story; that they weren't mere observers, but rather, participants in the plot. He had the foresight to appreciate the advantage of having a guest come to a physical attraction. Unlike traditional rides like the carousel or roller coasters in amusement parks, the visitor's presence is acknowledged. Not only that, but the guest had a role to play. Now that's good storytelling!

In thinking about your visitor flow, consider how the story unfolds from one space to the next. Take a shot at the big idea of each scene and write them down for each bubble.

The Haunted Mansion attraction is the perfect example of telling one story at a time per scene/room.

SCENE BREAKDOWN:

The Foyer

Guests meander through a creepy courtyard before arriving inside a dark foyer where candles flicker and an unseen organ plays a haunting tune. The voice of a "Ghost Host" welcomes its visitors, beginning with the now famous words, "When hinges creak in doorless chambers...."

The Story — Welcome to this spooky mansion.

Portrait Gallery (The Stretching Room)

The Ghost Host continues speaking as the guests enter a dimly lit portrait gallery and the secret panel slides shut, disappearing into the wall. The room stretches, revealing morbid, but also comical portraits, of former residents. The Ghost Host challenges us to find a way out of the doorless and windowless chamber. Of course, there's always *his* way.

The Story — Find a way out.

Portrait Hallway

Guests walk out into a hallway where they find a series of portraits revealing a haunting outcome. At the end of the hallway, they find white carved faces of busts that seem to follow them. Then the guests arrive at the moving platform of black "Doom Buggy" vehicles to take them on the rest of their "visit."

The Story — You're being watched.

Endless Hallway

After climbing a Grand Staircase, the journey continues as guests pass by a dark and misty hallway that reveals hidden wings of the mansion. Guests pass a creepy suit of armor, a candelabra floating in a hallway, door knockers banging, glowing eyes, skeletal hands behind doors, and a ghostly clock spinning uncontrollably.

The Story — You're going deeper and deeper into the mansion.

Conservatory

Guests observe a casket of a recently deceased member of the mansion's family. The skeletal hands of the deceased try to open the casket lid as he cries out to be released.

The Story — There is no escape.

Séance Circle

Guests enter a circular room where a séance is taking place. A glowing crystal ball floats in the air with a ghostly apparition of the face of a medium, Madame Leota. She chants mysterious incantations while objects and musical instruments float around the room.

The Story — You're entering a spiritual world where anything can happen.

The Ballroom

Guests climb a walkway and witness a ghostly party in a grand ballroom. Despite being dead, the ghosts seem to be having a grand old time; blowing out candles on a cake, dancing, eating, drinking, singing, and dueling.

The Story — Come join us.

Attic

Guests enter the attic filled with trunks, antiques, portraits of dead grooms, and other forgotten items. This is the private haunting ground of a long dead bride, whom we meet at the end of the room.

The Story — Not every story ends in "happily ever after."

Graveyard

Guests exit the mansion and enter the graveyard where they encounter all manner of ghosts singing "…grim grinning ghosts come out to socialize.…"

The Story — We may be dead, but we're grinning. (In other words, "Don't feel sorry for us. It's not so bad being dead.")

Mausoleum Entrance (Hitchhiking Ghosts)

As guests enter the mausoleum and leave the graveyard behind, three ghosts are standing, looking to hitchhike. Guests see their reflection in a mirror and seated next to them is one of the hitchhiking ghosts, ready to follow them home.

The Story — We may follow you home.

Mausoleum Hallway

As guests move down a walkway, they come upon a physical manifestation of "Little Leota" who gives them a haunting message: "Hurry back, hurry back! Be sure to bring your death certificate if you decide to join us … make final arrangements now … we've been dying to have you."

The Story — You're *always* welcome back.

By telling one story at a time per scene/room, the Haunted Mansion successfully breaks down the guest journey in engaging and dramatic chapters, while still maintaining the emotional hook of "family fun spookiness." Notice how the journey never gets too scary. Guests are given "breaks" between moments of scariness by enjoying more light-hearted and, often times, comical moments.

A good story has peaks and valleys, meaning that it's not consistently focused on one "feeling." There is a "driving feeling" throughout the experience, but your audience could very well experience a spectrum of emotions. Ultimately, you want your audience to be emotionally moved by your experience, and hopefully, changed by the experience.

RESEARCH TRIPS

During a charrette, you may be fortunate enough to travel with your team to the project's location or to destinations that will bring inspiration to your project. My projects have taken me all over the world, from Beijing to Orlando. Often times, these trips are a way to meet and collaborate with the client team and immerse yourself in their culture, company, and environment.

I remember traveling to Beijing and Shanghai while working with BRC Imagination Arts to meet with experts in the telecommunications industry as we were working on the Information and Communications Pavilion for the 2010 Shanghai World Expo. We visited with the Shanghai Dianxin (Telecom) Museum, met with representatives from China Mobile and China Telecom, and even interviewed multiple generations of people in their homes regarding their cellphone usage. It was a research and fact-finding mission, as well as an inspirational trip. We had to immerse ourselves in the country, culture, and lifestyle to paint an authentic picture of China's history and future of telecommunications.

POST-CHARRETTE

After the charrette and research trip, the team returns to their respective offices and work spaces to start developing their work. The designers start their designs, the artists begin illustrating storyboards and other key scenes, the writers start writing, and the creative director ensures that everyone has what they need for their next steps into the concept/design phase.

The writer's work is to make sure that all of the big ideas captured in the charrette will now be integrated into the story of the experience. Working closely with the creative director, the writers serve as the "narrative glue" between all of the disciplines, to ensure that everyone is designing to one holistic experience. This is when the writer starts developing answers to the fundamental questions.

THE BIG QUESTIONS

IMMERSIVE STORYTELLING QUESTION (ISQ) WHEEL

Like any good story, the writer/storyteller must ask the Why, What, Who, When, Where, and How of the experience. This method of inquiry can be traced back to Aristotle's work on ethics, which helps to understand the "elements of a circumstance." Although Aristotle developed his system to examine the voluntary or involuntary action of a person,[10] many people have used this method to explore the particular elements of a story. Journalists, the police, and investigators use this in their research, reporting, and writing to paint a full picture of a particular circumstance.

We can also apply this useful tool in immersive storytelling with a simple diagram I call the "Immersive Storytelling Question (ISQ) Wheel." If we're using a bicycle wheel as the analogy, the WHY of the experience is the focal point (the hub) in the wheel, as it informs every other element, especially the WHAT, WHO, WHERE, and WHEN (the spokes). The HOW (rim) serves as the wrapper to the experience which begs the question of how visitors will

---

[10] Aquinas, Thomas (1952). Sullivan, Daniel J. (ed.). *The Summa Theologica. Great Books of the Western World.* Translated by Fathers of the English Dominican Province. Encyclopedia Britannica. pp. Q7. Art. 3. Obj. 3.

experience your story, as well as how your visitors will feel. Each of these elements can be further divided into more questions. Together, every element has an important part to play in the entire story experience.

I'll discuss each of these elements in more detail. Each of these elements may have more than one question (and ultimately, definition), so it's up to you to decide which of these questions you'd like to consider for your experience wheel.

ISQ WHEEL

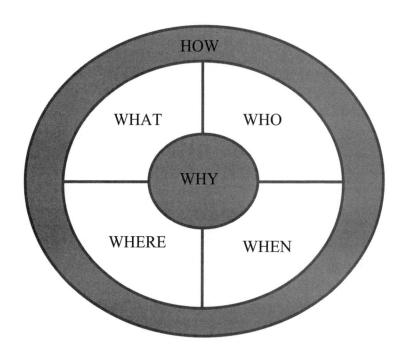

IMMERSIVE STORYTELLING QUESTIONS

These are the questions I pose for every experience. Here, I've grouped them into their categories, but in the following chapters, I will approach each of these questions in a different order than listed below.

WHY
- Why share this story with the world?

WHO
- Who is your audience?
- Who are the characters in your story?

WHAT
- What is the transformation you want to create in your audience?
- What is your theme?
- What is the wish fulfillment of your story?
- What are the mood and tone of your experience?
- What is the role of your audience?
- What are the rules of engagement?
- What are the emotional anchors of your experience?
- What are the comparables?

HOW
- How will your audience feel?
- How will your audience experience your story?

WHERE
- Where is the authenticity in your story?
- Where is your story set?

WHEN
- When does your story take place?

WHY SHARE THIS STORY WITH THE WORLD?

"Just as the brain detects patterns in the visual forms of nature — a face, a figure, a flower — and in sound, so too it detects patterns in information. Stories are recognizable patterns, and in those patterns we find meaning. We use stories to make sense of our world and to share that understanding with others. They are the signal within the noise. So powerful is our impulse to detect story patterns that we see them even when they're not there."

— Frank Rose, "The Art of Immersion: Why Do We Tell Stories?"[11]

As I mentioned in the previous chapter, the WHY of the ISQ Wheel is the most important question to ask. The answer is what will hold your experience together. As the storyteller, you must understand the meaning of your story. What's the message you're trying to convey about life and the human condition?

Answering the WHY starts your journey to build the core foundation and narrative thrust of your story. The narrative thrust compels your audience to move forward in your experience in an emotionally compelling and dramatic way. The process is very similar to screenwriting, but so much more complex, because you have to engage all of the senses in, often times, a non-linear format. The secret to engaging your audience is to understand how your experience will make them feel.

As designers are purposeful in their design, so too, must storytellers be purposeful in their story. An architect doesn't randomly place a brick on a building. A designer doesn't randomly place a design element in their work.

---

[11] https://www.wired.com/2011/03/why-do-we-tell-stories/

Writers must be just as purposeful in selecting their theme, world, characters, activities, and other story elements in order to give it meaning. Everything should belong in the experience. They are parts of a whole that support the theme of the story. They belong because they support and add important layers to the greater story. If a design element doesn't support the theme, then it doesn't belong in the experience.

Purposeful storytelling signals to your audience that your story is intentional and every detail is not randomly included. It shows that the design of your experience isn't merely superficial "eye candy" for fun selfies and social media posts, but rather, one that speaks to a greater purpose. With purpose, you have meaning, and with meaning, you have change.

> *"If you want somebody to change their mind ... you've got to reach the heart."*
>
> — *Jane Goodall*[12]

To help explore the question of why you want to share your unique story, you must understand why we tell stories in the first place. There are plenty of reasons why we tell stories. We tell stories to inform and educate. We tell stories to heal. We tell stories because we don't want to feel alone. We want to share our experiences with others so that *they* don't feel alone. We want to connect with others and feel like we belong. We want to make sense of the world. We want to find meaning in our lives. We want to pass down stories to future generations. We tell stories

---

[12] https://www.forbes.com/sites/francesbridges/2020/04/30/jane-goodall-champions-pragmatism-for-progress-in-national-geographic-documentary-jane-goodall-the-hope/?sh=67b3df241d3c

because we will die one day. Stories, that if not told, may wither and be forgotten. We tell stories to be empathetic. By putting ourselves in the shoes of another person, we see a story unfold through another person's eyes. Last but not least, we tell stories to create a change in our audience. We tell stories to inspire and empower them.

As a storyteller, you have the power to influence your viewers and visitors. You can shape a generation. You can change a mindset. You can motivate people to do what they thought was impossible. You can inspire people to pursue their passions. You can educate the ill-informed and empower the helpless. A powerful emotional story can do anything.

As a storyteller, you want to reveal and share something with the world that is important and unique enough to warrant your audience's time (and money). In addition to creating something unforgettable and compelling, you should aspire to tell a story that is meaningful to your audience. If you believe that you have the power and responsibility to change, influence, and inspire the minds of your audience, you can take your storytelling to a higher level. You can change the world, one person at a time.

The Peranakan Museum (Singapore)

I visited the Peranakan Museum[13] in Singapore for the first time a few years ago, based on a recommendation from a friend. I didn't really know what to expect since many of the museums I visited in Singapore were interesting, but not very meaningful to me. That was until I visited the Peranakan Museum. The Museum's website describes

---

[13] https://www.nhb.gov.sg/peranakanmuseum/

itself as a museum that "explores the culture of Peranakan communities in Southeast Asia, and possesses one of the finest and most comprehensive collections of Peranakan objects." Peranakan is an Indo-Malay word which means "descendent," "native-born," or even "cross-breed." Anak means "child" in Bahasa Indonesia.

What is Peranakan history? Chinese traders were already flocking to Malaya (the Malay Peninsula and the island of Singapore) since the 10th century; but it was really in the 15th century when the Chinese emperor reopened Chinese-Malay trade relations, that large numbers of mainland Chinese traders permanently migrated to this region. Most of these traders married local women, and their children grew up in households that were neither fully Chinese nor Malay nor Indonesian, speaking more than one language. Over the next few decades, a unique culture emerged which combined Chinese and local traditions, cultures, and cuisines. The offspring of these Chinese traders and local women are known as the Peranakans.

Why was this museum experience meaningful to me? Because I'm an Indonesian-born, Chinese-American woman. On my mother's side, at least four generations of my family were already living in Indonesia. My maternal great-grandfather came from China to marry a "local woman," my great-grandmother. My maternal grandmother and her siblings were the first Peranakans in our family.

This museum spoke to me in so many ways. For the first time in my life, I went to a museum that told my history. I've been to Indonesian history museums, Chinese history museums, Chinese-American history museums, and American history museums. The Peranakan Museum was unique because it told the story of a specific group of people that were straddling multiple cultures. It was the first time I saw people that looked like me hanging on the walls. The experience struck me with such a strong sense of belonging. I understood and appreciated what it meant to be Peranakan and felt a swelling sense of pride. The experience changed me and my outlook. I didn't feel excluded anymore because this museum represented my people's history. I didn't feel like an outsider in this experience. It brought a mirror to my face and said, "Look, this is who you are." (Please see the color photo section.)

HOW WILL YOUR
AUDIENCE FEEL?

*"The best and most beautiful things in the world cannot be seen
or even touched. They must be felt with the heart."*

— *Helen Keller*[14]

The first HOW question of the ISQ Experience Wheel
asks the very important question of how your audience
will feel. Your audience enters your experience feeling
a certain way. This is their status quo, which represents
their ordinary lives and original mindset. As they enter
the experience, hopefully their feelings start to change.
In the middle of the experience, perhaps they are moved
to question or wonder or imagine. What does it mean to
influence what your audience will feel?

Think about the last favorite film you watched. How did
certain characters make you feel? How did certain scenes
make you feel? Did some of the characters and situations
stay with you long after the movie ended? Have you ever
wondered why? Maybe they resonated with you in some
meaningful way. Maybe the film provoked something
inside you that had never been provoked before. Maybe it
reminded you of someone or something. Maybe it simply

---

[14] https://quoteinvestigator.com/2012/07/18/best-not-seen/

asked the question, what if that were me? What would I do in that situation?

A well-told story should feel like an emotional roller coaster. There are highs and lows in emotions that make you think about your own life. They also help us to empathize with other people's stories by experiencing their lives in a safe way without real-life consequences.

Feelings aren't reserved for movies. We experience emotions in every compelling place we visit, from national parks to theme parks. Here are examples of some of the experiences and the emotions related to them.

Haunted Mansion in Disneyland	— *Playfully Scared*
Disney California Adventure Park's Redwood Creek Challenge Trail	— *Adventurous*
Musee Marmottan Monet	— *Inspired*
Anne Frank House	— *Enlightened*
Yosemite National Park	— *Awestruck*
National Museum of African American History and Culture	— *Empowered*
Museum of Jurassic Technology	— *Curious*

Thinking about how you want your audience to feel is one of the most important questions you can ask in designing your experience, because it helps establish the tone of your experience, which we will discuss in a later section. There should really be one word to describe how you want your audience to feel — curiosity, fear, happiness, sadness, even anger and disbelief. It can be a noun or an adjective. For *Star Wars: Galaxy's Edge*,[15] I used the word anticipation.

Portfolio Creative Executive, Scott Trowbridge, responsible for the *Star Wars* portfolio at Walt Disney Imagineering, asked us a very important question at the beginning of the project. He asked us, we know what *Star Wars* is, but what does *Star Wars* mean to us? By us, he meant the most important people who would experience this land — our guests.

Super fans have waited over forty years to walk into a physical, immersive, authentic land that represented their wildest *Star Wars* fantasies. Their anticipation is palpable. We design with them in mind, first and foremost. We wanted our fans to be filled with so much awe and anticipation, that they would move excitedly from corner to corner to see every single detail of Black Spire Outpost. We wanted the audience to keep exploring, fueled by their burning anticipation.

When thinking about how your visitors should feel, consider their level of familiarity with the subject or the world you're designing. We considered all levels of fandom, from the guest who knew nothing about *Star Wars* to the super fans who could point out every "Easter egg" in the land and know its origin. We wanted everyone to feel great anticipation for the next activity in the land. We wanted our guests to have a great sense of discovery. This feeling was manifested in every aspect of the design, from the rides to the architecture to the retail experience to the smallest details like blaster holes on the walls.

---

[15] https://disneyland.disney.go.com/destinations/disneyland/star-wars-galaxys-edge/

Museum of Jurassic Technology (Los Angeles, CA)

I had no idea what to expect when I first visited the Museum of Jurassic Technology[16] in Culver City, a city within Los Angeles. All I knew was that it was a "strange little museum," based on a recommendation from a co-worker. He described it as the "anti-museum museum." I didn't understand what he meant until I visited the Museum for the first time. Even when you first walk through the non-descript door and enter the front desk/gift shop in a dimly-lit space, you are struck with wonder and curiosity.

The first question that popped into my head remained with me throughout the experience — what is this place? More questions started to fill my head as I continued on my journey into this peculiar place. Is this a museum? Is this an art gallery? Is this an experience of walking into a cabinet of curiosities? What am I looking at? Why is this here?

This curious place provoked many questions. It was a place that asked you to pay attention to things. It asked you to look at things (or a combination of things) that would never be spotlighted in the outside world. Whether the object was positioned behind a glass case, observed through a microscope, hung on a wall, or delicately displayed inside a glass orb, the visitor is invited to take a closer look. It truly was a cabinet of curiosities. For me, it perfectly captured the feeling of having just discovered an attic of odd things that once belonged to an eccentric individual. From art that can only be viewed through a microscope to taxidermized animals coupled with thought-provoking captions, everything you think you knew about museums or art galleries is questioned.

---

[16] https://mjt.org

By the end of the experience, I questioned why anything would be hung on a wall or displayed behind a glass case. After all, who determines what is worthy of being placed inside a museum? The experience posed a subjective perspective in which we, the audience, accept an object willingly as "art" or "something of value" and worthy of our attention. Should we accept that curation blindly or should we question and wonder?

One of my favorite spaces in the museum is a small terrace courtyard where you can serve yourself biscuits and tea. I'd like to think that this courtyard serves as a place of contemplation inspired by what you have just observed. The museum was so otherworldly and unique that it made me feel the thrill of having traveled to a different country. It captured my childlike wonder as I observed and discovered things for the first time. It made me stop and pay attention to everything around me.

Divination Table from the exhibit, The World is Bound with Secret Knots — The Life and Works of Athanasius Kircher, 1602–1680. Photo courtesy of Museum of Jurassic Technology.

WHO IS YOUR AUDIENCE?

*"I think it's what we've always tried to do, is just find
a unique way in, and find a unique way to be true to
what the character is from the comics and what fans
are aware of and expecting. And at the same time do it
in a way that mainstream audiences and as wide an
audience as possible can find their own way into it."*

— *Kevin Feige*[17]

The most important WHO question in your ISQ Experience Wheel is none other than the hero of the journey — your visitor. Everyone else takes second stage, even the characters of your story.

Similar to writing for a movie, a television series, or a speech, you should always know your audience. More specifically, your target audience. You will design your experience to be enjoyable for all audiences, but if your experience has a unique story that will strongly resonate with the super fans, then you should focus your story to that specific group of people first and foremost. Present your story well to the target audience and the rest will follow.

In the museum industry, there is the idea of "streakers, strollers, and students," terms coined by George MacDonald (a former museum director) in the 1990s. Streakers

---

[17] https://collider.com/ant-man-kevin-feige-talks-expanding-mythology-avengers-more/

move quickly through exhibitions and gather general impressions about the place, but never get influenced or impacted by the experience. They visit the Louvre Museum to see the *Mona Lisa* and maybe some of the other "greatest hits" of the collection to check it off their list, but aren't interested in much else.

Strollers take their time to stop for a few minutes at each point of interest, absorb a little piece of information and maybe learn something new. They may move from one thing to another based on what catches their interest, but they never stay long enough to absorb every single detail. Many children fall into this category. Like bees, they'll move from one flower to the next, get what they can from it, and move on. They'll pay enough attention as long as it holds their interest, but move on when it no longer does.

Students (which have since been termed scholars) stay the longest to study and observe every last detail. The scholars are super fans in theme parks. They're not only familiar with the subject matter, they are passionate about it. Perhaps even more passionate than the designers themselves! In a museum, they read every single text on a caption, absorb the information, and reflect on what they've learned. They're methodical in their approach of experiencing the museum and are diligent about ensuring they have learned all that they can about a topic.

Ultimately, you want to consider how can you design an engaging experience for each of these visitors. The more interest you can create among these different groups of visitors, the more likely you will create a successfully engaging experience.

RESPECT THE SCHOLARS

Let us imagine that you're designing an exhibit about "The 100 Greatest American Movies of All Time." If you work backwards and start with the scholars, how would you design an experience for the movie fanatic (your target audience)? They are the ones who will validate the content and presentation of your exhibit. You would bring in some of these scholars in the blue sky process. Blue sky is the stage in which brainstorming and big ideas occur. This early stage allows you to dream big and come up with your biggest and best ideas. These scholars serve as your sounding board and advisory council. They will suggest some great ideas that will make your exhibit credible.

Scholars, however, are not storytelling experts in the field of museum design or immersive experiences. They may be able to go into depth on the subject matter by helping you develop the what (What films are considered the greatest?), the why (Why are these films the greatest?), and the when (When were these films made?), but they won't necessarily understand the how (How should we tell this story?). The how is where you come in as a writer and storyteller.

I can't emphasize enough the importance of research. As a writer, you have the power and responsibility to tell a story that is truthful, accurate, and whole. As the storyteller, you have the unique and privileged opportunity to look at a subject from an unbiased point of view. You have the ability to inspire, inform, and change an audience mindset.

In considering the 100 best American films of all time, you have the responsibility to determine how comprehensive and inclusive these films are. What factors are you using to determine the "greatness" of these films? Will you consult with the American Film Institute, universities, and other notable organizations? In addition to the advice from your scholars, who and what else are you bringing in to inform your decision? Read about film history, interview filmmakers, speak with other experts in the field, watch the films, and know enough about the subject to have an informed opinion about it.

Perhaps you would consider factoids and "behind-the-scenes" information that could not be found in books or other media. Perhaps you would consider doing exclusive interviews with the screenwriters and directors to showcase in your exhibit. Scholars coming to your exhibit are looking for in-depth information and content that they would not gain anywhere else. They are searching for more details and nuances to fill their ever-flowing well of knowledge in the subject. As a writer and storyteller, you can challenge yourself to create content and experiences that give these scholars fuel to immerse and perhaps express themselves in their passion even further.

FROM STREAKER TO STROLLER TO SCHOLAR

I have a confession. Often times, when I'm pressed for time or if a subject doesn't draw me as much, I begin as a streaker in an experience. I go through an exhibit or experience with the mentality of "Okay, what's this about? Will this be interesting to me? Why should I care?" I'll walk briskly from space to space with a somewhat open mind in the beginning of the experience, but if it doesn't hook me in the first couple of minutes, then I continue streaking through the exhibit without paying much attention.

Time is my most precious commodity, and if the experience doesn't entice me from the start, then I'll find something else to do with my time. It's like picking up a new book. If it doesn't pull me into the world in the first chapter or two, then I close the book and never pick it up again. If you can't hook your audience almost immediately, then you're going to lose them.

However, there are experiences that have changed my mind about a topic of interest. I transform from streaker to stroller because of the experience's ability to influence me to care about the topic. This is why asking the question of "Is this story worth sharing?" is very important in developing an experience. If it is a story worth telling, then you have the potential to change someone's mind about what they think they know about a story or topic.

The ultimate goal as a storyteller would be to change a streaker into a scholar. A visitor may come in with little to no interest about the experience, but when they leave, they are influenced and transformed. They may leave wanting to learn more about the story or subject, and eventually become a fan.

The ability to influence and perhaps even to change someone's mindset about a story, idea, and/or subject matter is a powerful notion. This is one of the reasons why we do what we do. We want to create meaningful moments and lasting memories for the whole family, no matter their level of interest or familiarity with a subject. If everyone walks away having learned something new and feeling moved, then we have done our jobs well.

WHAT IS THE TRANSFORMATION YOU WANT TO CREATE IN YOUR AUDIENCE?

Here comes the first WHAT question in your ISQ Experience Wheel. What is the change you want to create in your audience?

The best stories change you. Think about the last great book you read or the last great film you watched. It stays with you. It lingers. It makes you think and ponder. That's what a good story should do. It should make you reflect on the human condition and make you feel less alone. A great story changes the world, one person at a time.

How do you create change in your audience? There are four ways you can increase your audience's likelihood to feel moved and be transformed.

1) TRUTH — Tell an emotional story that embraces universal truths.

2) PERSONAL — Make it personal.

3) STATUS QUO — Meet your audience where they are.

4) COMMUNITY — Create a world where they can connect with others.

I'll break each of these points down further.

1) TRUTH — Tell an emotional story that embraces universal truths.

In designing your experience, your aim is to welcome all types of visitors regardless of their ethnicity, nationality, gender, race, religion, age or sexual orientation. Age may be a factor if the content of the exhibit is for mature audiences only, or if the format is inaccessible to young children (e.g., height restrictions). With that said, the one commonality between all of us is that we are all human. We are humans who have experienced the entire spectrum of emotions in our unique lives. What we have in common is that we all feel happy, sad, angry, jealous, curious, excited, and overwhelmed, no matter who we are and where we're from.

A universal truth can be defined as something that will apply to any human, no matter who they are or where they come from. A good example of a universal truth is the pursuit of love and happiness. Who wouldn't want to find love and connect with another person? Who doesn't want to feel less lonely?

Not all universal truths are positive. They can include acts of jealousy, revenge, ambition, and greed. Shakespeare understood this well when he wrote his many comedies and tragedies. His stories have withstood the test of time and resonated over the centuries to people all over the world. His stories are easily understood, in spite of who we are. There is a character or a story we can all relate to.

One of my favorite universal truths is the strong human need to protect their own. I love to ponder: What would you do for the ones you love? How far would you go to protect them? These questions have prompted some of the greatest stories in literature and entertainment, from Cormac McCarthy's post-apocalyptic novel *The Road* to the Disney animated film *Frozen*. A father's love for a son will send him to extreme measures to protect his innocent child. A sister's love knows no bounds, even if it means risking her own life to save her sister's.

In creating your story, remember to embrace these universal truths so that your experience is emotional, compelling, and dramatic. There is no drama without emotion. This is directly related to how you want your audience to feel during your experience. Tell a story based on universal human truths so that we may experience the same emotion.

By discovering the universal truth of your experience, you answer the question of why this experience matters and why it should exist in the world. This directly influences why your audience should care about your story. Despite your audience's varied backgrounds, if you embrace a compelling universal truth, then everyone who goes through the experience will feel moved and transformed.

National Museum of African American History and Culture (Washington, D.C.)

One of the best examples of a museum that embraces universal human truths is the National Museum of African

American History and Culture[18]. During my experience in the Museum, I was so moved and empowered, in ways that I've never experienced in a museum of African-American history before.

The Contemplation Court at the Smithsonian's National Museum of African American History and Culture. Photo: Margaret Kerrison.

The experience started from the bowels of a slave ship (the underground level), and proceeded to take me through the emotional milestones of African-American history (a history you'd be hard-pressed to find in any one textbook). What was so compelling about the construction of this museum was that as a visitor, you literally climbed higher up the building as the timeline progressed. The experience started in a slave ship (where you felt trapped, claustrophobic, vulnerable) and you ended up at the bright and airy top of the museum floor where you felt

---

[18] https://nmaahc.si.edu

hope and optimism as you were surrounded by the lives and accomplishments of African-American heroes. The story is one of hope and optimism, even though its history is rooted deep in unfathomable horrors. It is an emotional story of the power of the human spirit. How despite the deep-rooted systemic racism prevalent in our country, African-Americans have risen to the challenge and continue to fight for their rights every day.

I walked away learning that American history is African-American history. As I moved from space to space, I experienced the universal human truths of the right to be free. Every human should have that right, regardless of gender, religion, creed, national origin, skin color, or socioeconomic status. It prompted questions and dialogue around race, racism, and other challenging topics. It asks many important questions based on universal truths: Does any person have the right to *own* another person? Does any person have the right to determine the fate of another person without their consent? Is one skin color superior to another? Who gets to make the rules? What are the repercussions of this history in present day America? How can we further educate ourselves in our own unconscious bias? What can we do to be an anti-racist? What can we do to change ourselves?

As humans inhabiting and sharing the same planet, we need to face history, no matter how dark and traumatic. Before we claim to know everything and pass any judgment, we must do our part as global citizens to learn about one of the most marginalized groups of people in this country. With knowledge, comes understanding and the commitment to be advocates for the African-American community.

2) PERSONAL — Make it personal.

The closer your audience is to a story, the more they will be affected by it. For most of us, watching the world news doesn't impact us as much as watching the national or local news. Something happening to someone on the other side of the world may not affect you as deeply as something that's happening across your street ... to some-one you know. How can you create a personal story for your experience?

The closer a story is to your audience, the more they believe it concerns them. This goes back to telling an emotional story that embraces universal truths. If we can't find any commonality with a story, at least we can all agree on the human condition. We all feel hungry, scared, happy, sad, jealous, and so on. How can you find the commonality and make your story personal, regardless of who your visitor is?

A PERSONAL STORY IS A UNIVERSAL ONE

"In the particular is contained the universal."

— *James Joyce*[19]

Let us imagine that we're working on an exhibit about the immigrant journey to the United States. We can choose to chronicle the entire history of the various groups of immigrants that have migrated into the country, and highlight key moments in which people's mindsets were changed and policies were made. But what if we focus on the emotion of the story? What could that look and feel like? What if we tell a story about a specific family of immigrants

---

[19] https://publishing.cdlib.org/ucpressebooks/view?docId=ft5s200743;chunk.id=d0e10921; doc.view=print

illegally coming into the country by crossing the border? A story about a family is something that we can all relate to, no matter where we're from. How can you put your audience into an immigrant family's shoes? How can you make them feel an emotion that is based on the universal human truth of family bonds?

Imagine that you've designed an exhibit which compellingly chronicles the harrowing journey that people must take in order to protect their rights, their lives, and their families when they have decided to leave their countries. Then imagine that in the final space of your experience, the audience enters a projection-mapped room or virtual reality area that gives you the opportunity to walk in the footsteps of a particular immigrant family.

Acclaimed film director, Alejandro G. Iñárritu, explored such a concept with his virtual reality installation *Carne y Arena (Virtually present, Physically invisible)*[20]. The moving installation explores the human condition of immigrants and refugees. Based on true accounts, Iñárritu places visitors in a twenty-minute solo journey that captures a fragment of an immigrant's story. This experience was so powerful, that in 2017, Iñárritu was presented a special Oscar for *Carne y Arena*, recognized by the Academy as an exceptional storytelling experience.

Inspired by Iñárritu's work to blur the lines between subject and bystander, let us return to our museum example. Following the journey of a specific immigrant family is powerful, but let's make it even more personal. Let's

---

[20] https://carne-y-arena.com

follow in your footsteps, as if you're an immigrant parent of two young kids.

We journey with you from a first-person perspective illustrating a pivotal day in your life. Perhaps you are getting ready for the final step in your journey. You are going to cross the U.S.–Mexican border with your two young children. You're in your home, packing your bags and belongings, making sure the kids' shoelaces are tied, making sure they have the right clothes on, that they have enough food and water.

You look back at your house, for the very last time. Your children are crying, but you tell them to be strong; that they will have a new home in America. That the most important thing is that they are together. You and your children travel to a house on the other side of Mexico by dangerously jumping on trains, hitchhiking on open bed trucks, and walking. You finally arrive at a discrete location, a house filled with other strangers and families and meet with the "coyote," the person responsible for taking you successfully across the border. You've sacrificed life and limb to get to where you are, crossing the border on dangerous terrain, in the blanket of the cold, dark night, with two young children in tow. Then just when you have the border in sight, you're captured by the United States Border Patrol. They take you to a facility, tear your children from your arms, and throw you alone in a holding cell.

HOW WILL THIS EXPERIENCE MAKE YOU FEEL?

By making the story personal, we can inspire change in our audience by making them feel. By walking in an immigrant's shoes, even for a few minutes, we can begin to understand what it could feel like to be an immigrant desperate to take her family across the border.

As your audience steps away from this experience, perhaps there's a dedicated space where they can reflect and share their thoughts. Perhaps they can read the thoughts of other people who have experienced it as well. You may prompt the audience with questions on how they felt or what they thought about the experience. Ultimately, you've tapped into their emotions by telling a personal story that embraces a universal human truth: Parents love and protect. They will do whatever it takes to take care of their family.

3) STATUS QUO — Meet your audience where they are.

In linear storytelling formats such as film and television, viewers are introduced to the protagonist in their status quo, meaning their "normal life" and "ordinary world," before their journey begins. Their status quo is their existing state or condition before a dramatic change occurs, propelling them into their journey.

In immersive storytelling, your audience *is* the protagonist. You have to meet them where they are, in their status quo, so they can begin their journey of change. How do you do that when everyone has a unique status quo? How can you begin to know what goes on in your audience's personal lives?

The best approach is to explore the status quo of your audience in the context of your experience. If you're doing a space adventure, are we all travelers originating from Earth? Will that be a common ground for all of us to begin our journey? Help your audience suspend their disbelief by meeting them as close as possible to their ordinary lives. In other words, don't make them work so hard to enjoy your experience.

The concept of meeting your audience where they are asks a couple of questions: 1) How do you make the experience inclusive of all visitors, regardless of who they are? and 2) How do you engage your visitors in a way that makes them *want* to be a part of your story? In other words, how do you create an experience that allows them to see themselves in this story? This relates back to telling a story with a universal truth and making the story personal.

I found that one of the most effective ways to meet your audience where they are is by looking within your own team for diversity of thought. In the *Star Wars: Galaxy's Edge* example, we had quite a range of fandom within our own team, from the team member who could read fluent Aurebesh (the written *Star Wars* language) to the team member who didn't know the difference between *Star Wars* and *Star Trek*. By building a team that represented all of the different "audience groups," we were able to socialize our ideas with one another and receive feedback on whether something was compelling or not, based on their familiarity with the franchise. This was a great way for us to try out new ideas and improve upon them (what we Imagineers call "plussing" an idea). If an idea didn't resonate with one group of people, then we had to figure out a way to make it more inclusive, so that we can ensure that they too felt excited about the idea.

In meeting your audience where they are, there's a better chance of changing your audience with your story. Rather than talking down to them, you should aim to communicate at *their* level of familiarity with the subject. However, what if your team members don't represent the audience that will visit your experience?

For example, what if the experience is targeted towards children? When I worked with BRC Imagination Arts on the *Journey to Mars: Explorers Wanted*[21] exhibit for the Kennedy Space Center Visitor Complex, our target audience was the future generation of NASA workers, more specifically, young children. How could we meet our audience where they are, based on their age group? We knew we had to make the experience educational, but also entertaining and FUN. (Please see color photo section.)

> *"If you can't explain it simply, you don't understand it well enough."*
>
> — *Albert Einstein (attributed)*[22]

In the *Journey to Mars: Explorers Wanted* example, the team had to ensure that the exhibit was simple to understand and fun for kids. Based on successes of other comparables within the NASA Kennedy Space Center Visitor Complex exhibits, as well as other space science exhibits around the country, we designed a space that was both informative and entertaining. We created a multimedia exhibit

---

[21] https://www.kennedyspacecenter.com/explore-attractions/nasa-now/journey-to-mars-explorers-wanted
[22] https://www.quotes.net/quote/9276

highlighting what was currently happening at NASA, and developed simple interactive games and simulations for kids to get a more hands-on approach to learning.

A few times a day, the exhibit space would turn dark and visitors would be encouraged to sit in the center of the space to watch a hosted show about NASA's plans to explore deep space. In the media show, we captured the excitement of working at NASA by highlighting the steps it took for a team to take the journey to Mars. The "cherry on top" was seeing the adults in their NASA roles transform into children. Kids can literally see themselves in the mission of exploring space. We meet them where they are.

Journey to Mars: Explorers Wanted, NASA Kennedy Space Center Visitor Complex. Photo: BRC Imagination Arts

As storytellers and designers, we often get too caught up with overthinking our ideas. We become so clever, crafty, or complex with our concepts that the project becomes inaccessible and complicated for our audiences. Sometimes your best ideas are simple ones. Above everything else, make the experience fun. It's not rocket science — except when it literally is.

4) COMMUNITY — Create a world where visitors can connect with others.

"The world is so empty if one thinks only of mountains, rivers and cities; but to know someone here and there who thinks and feels with us, and though distant, is close to us in spirit, this makes the earth for us an inhabited garden."

—*Johann von Goethe*[23]

As humans, we crave meaning in our lives and strive to find connection with people who see us for who we are without expectation or judgment. We want to know that others will make time and pay attention to us in a way that's sincere and truthful. As we get older, we get busier, and our lives are filled to the brim with household chores, work responsibilities, and social expectations. When visitors come to an immersive experience, they are carving out time in their busy lives to feel something and connect with others in a genuine way.

Immersive experiences serve as "therapy" of sorts. Feelings are heightened because people are not only given permission, but are encouraged to openly express themselves. In your experience, you want to create a setting where your visitors can be free to embrace and celebrate their wildest fantasies, all within the context of your world. What elevates your experience is the opportunity to build that compelling setting that allows like-minded people to find one another. They connect because of their shared affinity to the brand, story, and world. They find their people. They create their "tribe" or community.

---

[23] https://www.clarendonhousebooks.com/single-post/2018/07/28/the-wisdom-of-goethe

Consider how you can create special events, products, experiences, and locations within your world that provide a platform for your visitors to engage in their ultimate fantasy. You can celebrate and reward their enthusiasm by creating incentives for them to return again and again. Provide an atmosphere built around food and drink in your world that encourages conversation around the table. Form membership clubs with exclusive access or features that promise a more premium experience. Explore ways in which people can have a voice in shaping how they connect and form their community. Offer activities for the whole family. Develop your own culture and "language." Explore monthly, seasonal, or annual events that bring your visitors together.

**With real connection, people finding meaning.
With meaning, comes transformation.**

In San Francisco's *The Speakeasy*, audience members are literally and figuratively transformed. They can come already dressed or pay to rent a fabulous Roaring Twenties ensemble, as they step into a remarkable world of the Prohibition era. Audience members are free to explore the casino, bar, cabaret, secret passages, and hidden rooms, as they interact with "flappers, floozies, gangsters, and bootleggers during a 'choose-your-own-adventure' immersive theatrical experience full of extravagance and spectacle."[24] For audience members who have paid a premium, they are cleverly integrated into the story as characters (complete in head-to-toe costume).

---

[24] https://www.thespeakeasysf.com

In creating an immersive Roaring Twenties "interactive theater," the designers considered the different levels of engagement for their audience members. Whether it's connecting with the cast of characters, interacting with the servers and dealers, or connecting with other audience members, the spirit of the Roaring Twenties is wonderfully captured in this vibrant experience that makes you feel like you're "part of the club." (Please see color photo section.)

It's no secret. People want to be seen. How can you create an experience in which they can see others, and more importantly, themselves?

WHAT IS YOUR THEME?

"A strong theme is always running through a well-told story."
— *Andrew Stanton*[25]

I previously mentioned the importance of finding your theme. Every good story has a strong theme, and often times, more than one theme. A theme is the anchor of your story. It answers the question of what your story is about on a deeper level. In other words, it's the message within the narrative which reflects the universal human truths. It can be overt or underlying, but it informs every decision you make about your storytelling. Ultimately, the theme gives the audience a reason for paying attention and adds depths and layers to your story that the audience should ultimately find fulfilling.

The most important aspect of finding a strong theme in your story is that it should reflect the human condition from your perspective; the perspective of the creator/ writer. What are you trying to convey? What is your belief? For example, you want to tell the story of the universal truth of first love. What is your perspective on love? The answer would differ depending on who you ask.

---

[25] https://medium.com/tell-me-a-story-grandpa/the-power-of-storytelling-d03bc3729017

In *Romeo and Juliet*, William Shakespeare had many themes, but arguably one of the strongest themes is that of first love. What is his belief regarding love? Perhaps it's in the words of one of his characters. "These violent delights have violent ends," says Friar Laurence when he tries to warn Romeo early in the play. The story powerfully illustrates the theme of the dangers and violence of love, especially young, first love. In the story of Romeo and Juliet, love is not hopeful, easy, or idealized — it is violent, chaotic, and dangerous.

In *Call Me by Your Name*, a novel written by André Aciman, this story of first love unfolds between an adolescent man and an adult man. The theme of this coming-of-age story is beautifully represented in the title as well as the story — that romantic attraction often involves a recognition of oneself in someone else.

These are just two examples of different themes reflecting the same universal truth. In designing your experience, ask yourself, what is your bigger, deeper message to your audience? What belief do you want to convey to your audience?

Here are some common story themes:

1) Good vs evil
2) Love
3) Redemption
4) Courage and perseverance
5) Coming of age
6) Revenge
7) Betrayal

8) Power and corruption

9) Individual and society

10) Isolation and belonging

11) Innocence and guilt

12) Faith

13) Friendship and Cooperation

14) Kindness and Compassion

15) Acceptance and Rejection

The themes listed above are only some examples. Within each of these themes, there are also sub-themes that can be further explored. You can even have more than one theme for your experience, but ultimately, there should be a core theme to your story.

How can these common themes manifest into design? You might think that establishing a theme is too ambitious for a themed experience, especially if it's small in scale or short in duration. Think again. Every good story comes with a strong theme. It is a chance for you to share a message with the world and tell them exactly what you believe as a storyteller.

Meow Wolf's *Omega Mart* in Las Vegas is another example of using a strong theme to create a compelling experience. On their website, they describe their destination as "an interactive, mind-bending art experience. Participants explore an extraordinary supermarket that bursts into surreal worlds and unexpected landscapes."

As Emily Montoya, one of Meow Wolf's cofounders and Omega Mart creative director, explained in a *Los Angeles Times* interview,

> "It's all about reinventing the mundane spaces and trying to get you to reengage with a sense of curiosity and possibility to remember to wonder," Montoya says. "We have these signs in Omega Mart where it's like, 'Attention shoppers! Did you forget something? Don't forget the ice. Don't forget the butter. Don't forget yourself.' That's the crucial thing to take away. We forget ourselves every day. We have the choice and the freedom to reengage with ourselves and the world around us, to remind us that we have the capacity to create infinite beauty and change."[26]

A theme gives your experience a bigger purpose; a belief for others to embrace and value. When your experience aligns with your audience's beliefs and values, then the result will be magical and transformational.

Avengers Campus (Anaheim, California and Paris, France)

When the team was developing the theme for the *Avengers Campus*[27], they were inspired by the stories of the Marvel cinematic universe. They kept circling around the idea of heroes and heroism (how we too can become a hero without being a superhero). They were inspired by how the Avengers always came together to thwart evil and the undeniable fact that they were always STRONGER TOGETHER.

The team loved the idea that each of us had something unique to contribute to the greater whole. They circled

---

[26] Martens, Todd. "Meow Wolf's Omega Mart is opening in Las Vegas in a pandemic. What to know." *Los Angeles Times*, February 17, 2021. https://www.latimes.com/entertainment-arts/story/2021-02-17/meow-wolf-omega-mart-covid-era-opening-las-vegas-in-pandemic.
[27] https://disneyland.disney.go.com/destinations/disney-california-adventure/avengers-campus/

around the theme of the "individual and society" and how one person can make a difference in a collective. They also played around with the idea of Spider-Man's theme of "with great power comes great responsibility." How can we, as heroes, be responsible for our actions to make the world a safer, better place? How do we play that heroic role in an awesome destination that belongs nowhere else except in the Marvel universe?

Avengers Campus at Disney California Adventure Park. Photo: Margaret Kerrison

The team asked these important questions for many months and kept revising and iterating on the theme. Ultimately, they finalized upon these principles:

> We are driven by *optimism* and believe that with great *power* comes great responsibility: the choice of how to use that power.

> When a person chooses to *share* their power to help others, they become a HERO.

> When a *diverse* group of Heroes embraces each other's individual powers, they become a TEAM.

> When a *Team* harnesses their power as one, they become STRONGER TOGETHER.

This was a fantastic mission statement for the Campus. It encapsulated so many of their ideas into the theme of the individual and society, but seen through the lens of the Marvel universe manifested into a Disney destination where the visitors played an active role.

WHERE IS THE AUTHENTICITY IN YOUR STORY?

The first WHERE question in the ISQ Experience Wheel is not one based on a physical location. Rather, it asks where you can find the truth in your experience. As designers, you often have to build your experiences from scratch, but how can you find the authenticity in your story so it doesn't feel "fake," forced, or contrived? It's one thing to visit a national park and be surrounded by the natural beauty that has always been there, but how do you create a meaningful and memorable experience with something that has never existed before?

You need to find the authentic anchor of your story. This authenticity can come in various forms: **location, object, personality, story world,** and **activity**. It's important to have *at least one* of these forms of authenticity so that your experience stems from a real and genuine place. The most successful experiences derive authenticity from all of these forms. Let's explore them one-by-one.

LOCATION — WHY HERE?

An experience is often rooted in the authenticity of a story's location. It makes the story even more compelling if your audience can stand in the very place where "it's all happening" or where "it all happened." Many historical sites, national park experiences, architectural wonders, unique houses, heritage landmarks, factories, and distilleries are all structures or locations specifically related to significant events, developments, or personalities.

Examples of experiences rooted in authentic locations are the 9/11 Memorial Museum, Anne Frank House, Basílica de la Sagrada Família, Bodie State Historic Park (ghost town), Hoover Dam, Elvis Presley's Graceland, George Washington's Mount Vernon, Luray Caverns, Xcaret Park, Tivoli Gardens, Hearst Castle, Underwood Family Farms, One World Observatory NYC, and Disneyland, Anaheim. Yes, Disneyland! Why? Because it was Walt Disney's original theme park. He personally oversaw the location, design, and attractions of this magical place. Another example of an experience rooted in an authentic location is one of my personal favorites, the House of Sampoerna, in Indonesia.

House of Sampoerna (Surabaya, Indonesia)

Located in my birthplace of Surabaya, the House of Sampoerna[28] is a tobacco museum, which also serves as the company's headquarters and working factory. Built in 1862, the compound was a former orphanage managed by the Dutch, hence the heavy Dutch-colonial style architecture. A preserved historical site, it was purchased in 1932 by Liem Seeng Tee, the founder of Sampoerna with the intent of it being used as Sampoerna's first major cigarette production facility.

I'm not a smoker and don't condone smoking, but the House of Sampoerna is so deeply rooted in history that

---

[28] https://www.houseofsampoerna.museum/about-hos

it's worth visiting. Not only can you visit this historical site and museum, but you can also observe the workers through a glass window as you look down upon the working factory floor. The workers hand-roll clove cigarettes with impressive speed and precision. Rows and rows of female workers perform in a harmonious symphony, as they work to ensure each product is hand-rolled, trimmed, and packaged perfectly. There's something inspiring about watching a very skilled person practicing (and perfecting) their craft. Their craft is poetic and mesmerizing. I'm in awe every time I watch the workers at House of Sampoerna. A packer can create as many as 200 packs of cigarettes per hour. When I asked why the workers are all women, a (female) manager kindly explained that they make a better working community, and that the social environment creates a more efficient workforce. I wondered how other companies can learn from that lesson!

Observing workers at House of Sampoerna. Photo: Jane Tjandra

At House of Sampoerna, you can also visit an engaging museum highlighting the history of the company in the backdrop of the city's history, an eclectic gift shop selling locally made products, a café that serves local delicacies, and a modest art gallery. Plus, they offer free city bus tours hosted in English.

As you visit the House of Sampoerna, you know you are standing in history. You are also witnessing the making of a product in a working factory. Never underestimate the power of an authentic location in sharing your story.

OBJECT — WHAT HAVE YOU COME TO SEE?

The story of your experience can be rooted in an authentic object (living or non-living) or a collection of objects. Great examples are zoos, aquariums, traveling exhibits, museums, natural formations, art galleries, and temporary exhibits. I have too many personal favorites in this category. They include the *King Tut — Treasures of the Golden Pharaoh* (traveling exhibit), the *Thorne Miniature Rooms* in The Art Institute of Chicago, the San Diego Zoo, the Singapore Night Safari, the Peranakan Museum (Singapore), the Museum of Modern Art (NYC), the National Museum of African American History and Culture (DC), and the Huntington Library, Art Museum, and Botanical Gardens (San Marino, CA).

Visitors come from all over the world to discover and explore authentic objects. Your experience is even more compelling if there is nowhere else in the world where visitors can go to see the same object(s). Consider the Hope Diamond in the National Museum of Natural History (Washington D.C.), the *Mona Lisa* in the Louvre Museum (Paris, France), or the *David* of Michelangelo in the Galleria dell'Accademia (Florence, Italy). The "main draw" of your experience is the object itself. Visitors come for that particular object, but they also have the opportunity to explore other objects in your experience. There's a reason and validation for their visit, but they walk away with so much more than they expected.

Experiences inspired by the intrinsic value of these authentic objects create a more meaningful time for your visitors. As the designer and storyteller, consider how you can create a place that transcends the object itself. How can you create a world that captures the spirit of your authentic object(s)?

PERSONALITY – WHO HAVE YOU COME TO SEE?

Never underestimate the power of a personality. We see the power of talent and personalities in sold out concerts and speaker events. We travel across the world to see our favorite personalities and some of us even travel with them to all of their events as roadies.

Visiting Santa Claus is one of the most obvious examples of an experience based on the power of a personality. We see this experience take shape in many different forms, from the very basic Santa visits in shopping malls to the more elaborate themed "Santa Claus houses" where visitors spend quality time with Santa in a themed house at the North Pole and receive a photo package and other Christmas treats.

The Disney princesses are another great example of what draws our visitors to our Disney parks every year. The promise of meeting and visiting their favorite Disney princess, take a picture with them, exchange a few words, and receive an autograph, is a powerful wish fulfillment. Children can meet their heroes and create special memories with them.

Like Santa Claus and Disney princesses, the personality can be fictional, but the personality can also be non-fictional. The personality can be living, but the personality can also be deceased. Take the Abraham Lincoln Presidential Museum (Springfield, Illinois), for example. Visitors come from all over the country to experience the story of Abraham Lincoln. They may not be seeing him in the flesh, but they are coming to experience the next best thing — to follow in his footsteps and experience his personal journey.

Authenticity based on a personality typically hinges on the audience's familiarity with the person. It's possible to create a new character (or characters) for your experience, but without another form of authenticity to draw your audience, it would be challenging to entice visitors. If you are introducing new character(s), you should consider how you can engage your audience before the experience opens.

STORY WORLD — WHERE DO YOU WANT TO ESCAPE TO?

Another way to anchor your story in authenticity is to create an immersive environment based on a beloved story or Intellectual Property (IP). *The Wizarding World of Harry Potter, Star Wars: Galaxy's Edge,* and *Super Nintendo World* are great examples of achieving full immersion in a story world. Even though the stories are fictional, the stories are authentic and true to the brand. A fan of any of these beloved franchises can feel the authenticity of the place because of the great attention to detail, the "Easter eggs," the in-story references, environment, characters, and other elements that make the place feel real and engaging.

Stormtrooper at *Star Wars: Galaxy's Edge* in Disneyland. Photo: Margaret Kerrison.

By creating an authentic environment of the world, you fulfill on the promise of the story. There's no better way to authenticate the story of your world than by bringing in the subject matter experts to help develop your story. Their participation not only brings the authenticity, it also adds credibility to your world. Imagine building a *Harry*

Potter land without J.K. Rowling's involvement or a *Star Wars* land without Lucasfilm's involvement. They can give a holistic understanding of what makes the story meaningful for audiences. Only by understanding the DNA of these story worlds can you even begin to create a world that captures its spirit.

The Wizarding World of Harry Potter™ at Universal Studios Hollywood. Photo: Jules Marvin Eguilos on Unsplash.

ACTIVITY — WHAT WILL YOU DO?

Last but not least, many experiences don't have any particular location, object, personality, or story world to anchor their authenticity. Instead, these experiences rely on an authentic activity. Some examples of these experiences include zoos and aquariums, adventure parks, water parks, and other destinations offering unique recreational activities like petting jellyfish, alligator feeding, zip lining, kayaking, and rock climbing.

Sprinkle Pool at Museum of Ice Cream New York City. Photo: Margaret Kerrison

Consider the whimsical experience, Museum of Ice Cream, which started as a pop-up location with a 200,000-person waitlist[29] and can now be found in permanent locations in New York City and San Francisco. The experience promises the main activity of eating ice-cream in a fun,

[29] https://www.inc.com/guadalupe-gonzalez/maryellis-bunn-museum-ice-cream-moic.html

pastel-colored world, but also involves jumping into a pool of sprinkles, going down a multi-story slide, and taking selfies in colorful backgrounds. Never underestimate the power of a fun activity (and the opportunity for unique selfies)!

SUMMARY

Ultimately, you want to find the authenticity in your experience so that it's rooted in something genuine. When you create for creation's sake and do not give much thought and attention to what makes a place feel "real" and "truthful," then you lose its significance. Every visitor craves meaning in a story. By rooting your experience in some form of authenticity, your visitors walk away happy, inspired, and hopefully, transformed.

WHAT IS THE WISH FULFILLMENT OF YOUR STORY?

Every experience should have one or more wish fulfillments. It's the promise of your experience. This may come in the form of a bucket list — what your audience can see, do, eat, drink, feel, and experience.

I touched upon the concept of "suspension of disbelief" in an earlier chapter. This is when the audience is willing to suspend their disbelief to enter your immersive, fictional world. For a moment, they are willing to step into your story, fully knowing that it's not real. You, as the storyteller, need to help them get there without requiring them to work hard for it. Your visitors are eager and willing participants in a story that hinges on fulfilling their fantasies. However, the promise of the world must meet their expectations.

In the *Wizarding World of Harry Potter*[30] (please see color photo section), a visitor wants to go through their wish fulfillment of becoming a gifted wizard or witch. They want to take the Hogwarts Express, visit Hogwarts Castle, explore Diagon Alley to find the iconic establishments like the Leaky Cauldron and Quidditch Quality Supplies, have a wand choose them at Ollivander's, and cast a spell with their wand.

---

[30] https://www.universalorlando.com/web/en/us/universal-orlando-resort/the-wizarding-world-of-harry-potter/hub

The Wizarding World of Harry Potter™ at Universal Orlando. Photo: Aditya Vyas on Unsplash.

In *Star Wars: Galaxy's Edge*, visitors want to visit a cantina, drink blue milk, pilot the *Millennium Falcon*, be in the middle of an epic battle between the First Order and the Resistance, escape a *Star Destroyer*, build a lightsaber, build a droid, and meet their favorite characters like Chewbacca, Rey, Kylo Ren, and stormtroopers.

Millennium Falcon at *Star Wars: Galaxy's Edge* in Disneyland. Photo: Margaret Kerrison

In Meow Wolf's *House of Eternal Return,* visitors want to explore and "get lost" in the world and uncover the mysteries of the story.

Meow Wolf's House of Eternal Return (Santa Fe, New Mexico)

The *Harry Potter* and *Star Wars* experiences are two examples from big franchises, but what if you're designing an experience that's original and still unknown by name? Consider what Meow Wolf did with *House of Eternal Return.*

The name of the experience already promises two things: a house that you can explore and an adventure in which you can return to many more times. This mind-bending, interactive, and playful experience fulfills our wish to be curious, explore, discover, and engage with a world unlike any other. It's an interactive and immersive art installation come to life, which begs the question — what if you can walk into a painting? What if you can interact with pieces of art (unlike a museum where you're not supposed to touch anything)? This fulfills the audience's wish of interacting with an art environment in the form of a massive indoor playground where you can discover surprising things.

There's something about tapping into your childhood dreams and memories in the *House of Eternal Return* that is satisfying and memorable. All of your childhood fantasies of going through portals a la *Alice in Wonderland* and ending up in fantastical realms can finally be fulfilled in this experience. What happens when you walk inside your fridge or into your fireplace? Where does it take you? The answer continually surprises you.

In addition to the *House of Eternal Return* and *Omega Mart,* Meow Wolf has since added a third location in Denver, Colorado, titled *Convergence Station* where you enter an "immersive psychedelic, mind-bending art and an underlying rich narrative as you take a journey of discovery into a surreal, science-fictional epic."[31] (Please see color photo section.)

In designing the story of your experience, ask yourself what is the wish fulfillment? What is the promise that you want to make for your audience? Then be upfront with the messaging, so that your audience can understand exactly what they'll be experiencing. You don't want to promise something that you don't plan on delivering.

Spyscape HQ (New York City)

Successful experiences don't merely provide opportunities for a visitor to fulfill the action of their wishes, they also promise the visitor to transform and become their fantasy. In *Spyscape HQ,* visitors undergo a "Spychology" program designed by a former Head of Training at British Intelligence to uncover their skills and potential as a spy.[32] The experience successfully integrates interesting characters, stories, and objects from the history of espionage, but also gives the visitor a chance to test their own skills in a gamified and personalized mission to uncover their inner spy. Interactive activities such as decoding, detecting lies, and surveilling, create opportunities for the visitor to become a spy in the safety of an interactive museum experience. They can even test their reflexes as they go through a laser tunnel and hit as many buttons as possible in 2.5 minutes.

---

[31] https://meowwolf.com/visit/denver
[32] https://spyscape.com

At the end of the experience, visitors receive a video of their spy profile and laser tunnel performance via e-mail. (Please see color photo section.)

Going through the experience, I couldn't help but feel like I had the rare opportunity to see the world through a spy's eyes, transform myself into a spy for the two hours I spent in the experience, and most importantly, believe (even for a moment) that I had the potential to become one.

WHAT ARE THE MOOD AND TONE OF YOUR EXPERIENCE?

Mood and tone help create the main idea of a story. The *mood* is the atmosphere of the story, and the *tone* is the writer's attitude towards the topic. Both are represented by the setting, characters, shows, attractions, dining establishments, merchandise locations, and other opportunities for audience engagement.

WHAT IS THE MOOD OF YOUR EXPERIENCE?

The mood is the feeling the audience gets when they first enter your experience. It is represented by the environment, which is one of the key components of your space's placemaking. If you've never heard of the term "placemaking" before, it's a term used in designing public and immersive spaces. It is a multi-faceted approach to the planning, design, and sustainment of spaces that is influenced by the characters who live, work, and/or play in a particular space. In other words, it's a people-centered approach to creating a strong sense of place.

In theater and filmmaking, you would call this idea the mise-en-scène, which literally means "placing on stage" in the French language. It involves the arrangement of scenery and stage properties in a play or film set, which includes everything in front "of the camera" — the actors, set design, props, and lighting.

In film school, we learned how to describe a scene before placing any characters within it. Consider the opening scene of the classic 1985 film *Back to the Future* written and directed by Robert Zemeckis. We pan around Dr. Emmett Brown's lab/work space before we meet him. We get an idea of who he is by setting the mood of his space. He's some kind of a mad inventor, messy, somewhat disorganized, and judging from his collection of clocks on the wall, is obsessed with time. He has a dog, drinks coffee, eats toast, and judging from the mound of uneaten dog food, both he and his dog have been gone for a while. In just the first few minutes of the film, we understand the mood of the world.

Expedition Everest — Legend of the Forbidden Mountain (Disney's Animal Kingdom)

"We go to the mountain for enlightenment, for self-realization, for adventure, for discovery. It's pregnant with meaning. When people see a mountain, they invest it with meaning. Not plot."

— *Joe Rohde*[33]

One of my favorite themed queues is *Expedition Everest — Legend of the Forbidden Mountain*[34] in Disney's Animal Kingdom, created by legendary Imagineer Joe Rohde and his talented team. You start your adventure by discovering an office of a fictional "Himalayan Escapes" travel agency, before progressing to a replica pagoda

---

[33] https://www.knowyourquotes.com/We-Go-To-The-Mountain-For-Enlightenment-For-Self-realization-For-Adventure-For-Discovery-Its-Pregnant-With-Meaning-When-People-See-A-Mountain-They-Invest-It-With-Meaning-Not-Plot-Not-Charact-Joe-Rohde.html
[34] https://disneyworld.disney.go.com/attractions/animal-kingdom/expedition-everest/

with holy figures. Next, you enter a garden, followed by a shop selling expedition equipment. Then you discover a "Yeti Museum" of sorts, which contains displays showcasing information on the Yeti and even a mold of a Yeti footprint. There are thousands of little details and authentic artifacts brought from Nepal to illustrate the idea that many trips were taken to Nepal and brought to this "museum" in the team's mission to find the elusive Yeti. Then you witness the artifacts from the "lost expedition."

Expedition Everest at Disney's Animal Kingdom, Orlando, FL. Photo: Margaret Kerrison

What is the mood created in this queue? The placemaking of the environment supports a mood of mystery. What is this Yeti, and who are the people trying to learn more about this elusive creature? You don't meet a single character in the queue, and yet it paints an illustrative picture of the story. You get a sense that this is a place of obsessed adventurers looking to uncover a mystery. You are surrounded by expedition gear, authentic items from Nepal, and other environmental details, that make you feel like you've been transported to Nepal in an immersive story that feels like an otherworldly adventure.

Consider the mood of your story. Is it dark and mysterious? Light and happy? Does it feel oppressive? Scary? Optimistic? Joyful? Magical? Then paint a picture of your environment using the set design, props, and other details to support your mood. Remember, as a people-centered design approach, it should represent the characters that live, work, and/or play there.

WHAT IS THE TONE OF YOUR EXPERIENCE?

Once you've established the mood of the experience, you need to consider the tone. This is your (or your client's) perspective and attitude towards the topic or story. Another way to think about tone is how you deliver words in your own voice.

Imagine telling someone, "You're the worst thing that ever happened to me." From reading these words alone, out of context, you can assume that this is a negative attitude from one individual to another. Consider, however, changing the tone of these words into an underlying context of "I love you." The meaning behind the words changes based on the tone. Actors learn how to do this when they deliver their lines through what they call "subtext." Their words are focused on the meaning and intention of the words rather than the words themselves.

Lost Spirits Distillery (Los Angeles, California and Las Vegas, Nevada)

The way in which you deliver the tone in your experience adds meaning and intention to your story. Consider the *Lost Spirits Distillery*[35] Tour in Downtown Los Angeles, which I had the opportunity to experience before they suffered a small fire and later rebuilt. The tour was redesigned after the fire, but what I remember from the original tour is a fantastical journey through something I knew very little about — distilling spirits.

This tour takes you through the distilling process, but in a "theme park" format, boat ride and all. For the curious mind (even if you're not a drinker), it opens up your mind to the world of distilling from an artistic as well as a scientific approach. Yes, you'll get your tastings, learn all about distilling rum, but you'll also get your boat ride and spin around the carousel after tasting rum from a porcelain teacup. How amazing is that! I am not a rum drinker, but the experience was so unique, that it made rum tasting enjoyable and accessible for anyone.

In the very last tasting, we sat around a table with our tour group (about twelve Imagineers), under a large tent set in a fun tropical setting inspired by the film *The Island of Doctor Moreau* (1977). The co-founder/CEO of the distillery, Bryan Davis, hosted our tasting, and patiently and passionately answered all of our questions. We discovered that he was a huge Disney parks fan and was inspired by many of our attractions, hence the design of his fabulous distillery tour experience.

---

[35] https://www.lostspirits.net

The experience ended, as expected, in the gift shop. What was unexpected, however, was that there were mini audio-animatronics of parrots serenading us. It was a delightful little show. At one point, one of the parrots malfunctioned, and the co-owner used a stick to bop its head to make it run again. I loved the candor of the experience.

What were the mood and tone of this experience? The mood of the tour was whimsical and experimental, a "Willy Wonka's factory meets rum distillery." The tone: "Isn't science fun and amazing?" Overall, I thought this experience was a great success. It never took itself seriously, which is a really refreshing tone for a distillery. What I appreciated about the *Lost Spirits Distillery* is that they practiced what they preached — science is messy, fun, experimental, unpredictable, and beautiful. Their experience was a successful manifestation of their mindset, and captured the mood and tone in a uniquely compelling way that made them stand out from the crowd. I can't wait to visit their newly built *Lost Spirits Distillery* in Las Vegas, which promises to be bigger and even better. (Please see color photo section.)

HOW WILL YOUR AUDIENCE EXPERIENCE YOUR STORY?

(BASED ON THE DESIRED ACTION OF YOUR AUDIENCE)

"Different themes inevitably require different methods of expression. This does not imply either evolution or progress; it is a matter of following the idea one wants to express and the way in which one wants to express it."

— *Pablo Picasso*[36]

In determining the medium of your experience, you need to consider your target audience, theme, wish fulfillment, and audience action of your story. You are "building the stage" for your experience, and creating action opportunities for your audience to engage with a story that fulfills their fantasy. You are answering the HOW of the ISQ Wheel.

Consider the medium of your experience with this simple formula.

Wishing + Doing = Becoming
(Wish Fulfillment + Action = Transformation)

---

[36] https://www.biography.com/artist/pablo-picasso

Understanding your audience's wish fulfillment will help you determine which action you want your audience to partake in your experience. Combine your audience's wish fulfillment with the action and your audience will be transformed. By *wishing* to do something and *doing* the action, they will ultimately come closer to *becoming* the role.

For example, in *Spyscape HQ* (New York City), the audience's wish fulfillment is to become a secret agent (wishing). Their action (doing) is decoding, performing a lie detection test, and other activities (doing), to ultimately become their own version of a spy (becoming).

Your audience can have more than one action. Do you want them to observe, discover, immerse, participate, and/or interact? How does the medium best support their action? Would your experience be more engaging as an interactive exhibit, immersive game, pop-up gallery, character encounter, media show, attraction in a theme park, restaurant, shop, walkthrough experience, or some other medium that doesn't yet exist? You might consider a combination of media.

Depending on the medium of your experience, consider what kind of narrative is appropriate for your audience. Will it be a traditional linear narrative where there is a chronological timeline with a clear beginning, middle, and end? Or will it be a non-linear narrative in which you jump around in the story sequence?

Many theme parks are set up as non-linear narratives in which the audience chooses their own adventure. Whether a visitor decides to go on a ride first or visit the stores, it's up to them to curate their perfect day. Once they're on a ride or attraction, however, often times the experience is pre-determined. There is a clear beginning, middle, and end. Some of these attractions are linear (e.g., traditional dark rides, roller coasters) and some are non-linear (e.g., playgrounds, temporary exhibits).

Many museum exhibits are designed as non-linear and exploratory experiences in which the visitor can decide which gallery room to enter first. It's designed to be enjoyed in multiple ways in varying amounts of time. Whether a visitor decides to stay for ten minutes or ten hours in a museum, the storytelling narrative is designed for flexibility.

There are pros and cons to different narrative types. Let us explore them.

LINEAR STORYTELLING NARRATIVE

A linear narrative is a great way to control the story of the audience experience. It's a sure way for you to guarantee that every visitor experience is the same. If your audience is entering in the same way (queue/pre-show) and experiencing the same attraction (main show), and exiting the same way (post show/gift shop), then you can design with a clear three-act structure. Many rides and attractions in theme parks follow this model. Many mission-based video games are also linear.

There is a repeatability factor in linear narrative experiences that is enticing for visitors, because they know exactly what they're going to get with each visit. You have to ensure that your experience is a finely-oiled machine that will perform to a high quality of standard with each visit. The disadvantage is that the narrative may eventually feel dated and predictable. It may also become irrelevant for future generations.

MULTI-LINEAR STORYTELLING NARRATIVE

Linear narratives can also be multi-linear, meaning that the visitors enter in the same manner, but can choose to go in another story direction separate from another visitor. They have the same beginning, choose among an option of narrative paths, and eventually end up in the same place. *Sleep No More* is an example of a multilinear narrative in which visitors start from the bar, choose which direction they want to follow, and end up in the same room for the final performance.

This format gives the advantage of visitor options. There's a repeatability factor that encourage your visitors to return for a different experience every time. The disadvantage is that you, as a storyteller, will have to create and support multiple storylines and possibilities that are equally compelling. There is also a greater chance of FOMO (fear of missing out) for the visitor. They may feel anxious about the possibility of not attending the "better" or more interesting event. They can never truly be present in the moment because of this anxiety.

NON-LINEAR STORYTELLING NARRATIVE

Non-linear narratives can start from different story points and end up in different story points. They may not have a clear beginning, middle, and end. Or they may have several beginnings, middles, and ends. The visitor has the freedom to choose how they want to experience your story according to their own preferred level of engagement as well as their own time commitment.

The advantage of the design is that visitors are encouraged to explore and discover, rather than follow a path. This type of design works great for a younger audience, large groups of friends/families, and also those who are there to explore in a new and surprising way. Many play structures, museums, science centers, festivals, and pop-up events have this kind of narrative.

The disadvantage of this design is that you can't predict and control your audience's story experience. There's a greater chance that your visitors may encounter decision fatigue, a term coined by social psychologist Roy F. Baumeister based on the Freudian hypothesis of ego depletion, and describes the emotional fatigue of becoming overwhelmed with choices and which causes people to make poor decisions[37]. There is also less control for you, as the storyteller, to ensure that each visitor is experiencing the most compelling and engaging journey.

IMMERSIVE ENVIRONMENTS

Lastly, many experiences have a themed, immersive setting, without a narrative. They focus on creating an environment or "open world" in which the visitor can immerse themselves without a specific story. This type of experience can be very enjoyable and memorable, such as the Museum of Ice Cream, now with permanent locations in San Francisco and New York City.

---

[37] https://roybaumeister.com

The advantage is that the experience isn't beholden to any specific story, so that you, as the storyteller, can instead focus on the tactile, visual, and auditory elements. What makes a space beautiful, fun, inviting, exploratory, and engaging without any specific story? This is a question that you can explore with your team by leaning in to the wish fulfillment of your audience.

For the Museum of Ice Cream, the wish fulfillment is to celebrate and enjoy all things ice-cream with the ones you love. What a great concept — to enjoy one of the most beautiful inventions in the world in a fun, immersive environment. The creator, Maryellis Bunn, didn't design an experience for people to just eat ice-cream, but also to dive into a pool of sprinkles and be immersed in all things ice-cream. It's a combination of ice-cream parlor, playground, and art installation. Start with the wish fulfillment and you can't go wrong.

As fun and memorable as an immersive environment can be, it doesn't necessarily inspire a change in your audience. The feeling, for the most part, is present and fleeting, but it doesn't influence your audience in a deep and meaningful way. However, not every experience needs to have profound meaning. It simply goes back to what kind of an experience you want to create for the world.

Here are examples of experiences with different mediums based on the desired action of the audience.

Stranger Things Drive-Into Experience (Los Angeles, California)

The Stranger Things Drive-Into Experience was a unique medium born out of the COVID pandemic. We know what drive-through restaurants and drive-in theaters are about, but what's a drive-into experience? Exactly as it sounds. You drive into an immersive experience which recreates memorable moments in the mysterious world of *Stranger Things* using props, performers, audio via your car radio, and snack options that immerse the audience in the comfort and safety of their own cars. The result is a unique experience that embraces the world of *Stranger Things* without jeopardizing the health and safety of the audience or cast.

With the success of this experience and the easing of COVID restrictions, *Stranger Things* now offers an immersive walkthrough experience[38] in New York City and San Francisco.

Medium: Drive-Into experience
Action: Drive, Immerse, and Observe

Sleep No More (New York City)

What do you get when you combine a retelling of Shakespeare's *Macbeth* with Alfred Hitchcock's film noir storytelling? Why, the immersive theatrical experience *Sleep No More*,[39] of course. Created by British theatre company Punchdrunk, you really have to experience it to believe it. Set primarily in a mysterious, dimly-lit, 1930s-era establishment called the McKittrick Hotel, the audience wanders through a series of rooms on multiple floors located inside a converted warehouse. The audience's actions do not influence the actions of the characters nor the outcome of the story, allowing the audience to freely

---

[38] https://strangerthings-experience.com
[39] https://mckittrickhotel.com/sleep-no-more/

explore the spaces within the allocated time (up to three hours). This new form of theater, which they call "promenade theater," mimics the feeling of becoming ghosts passing through walls as the audience partakes in a voyeuristic adventure in this creatively haunting tale. (Please see color photo section.)

Medium: Immersive Promenade Theater
Action: Walk, Discover, and Observe

Noah's Ark (Skirball Cultural Center, Los Angeles, California)

A wonderful concept of an indoor playground themed around the story of Noah's Ark and utilizing found and repurposed everyday objects, Noah's Ark[40] is a delight for kids of all ages. An 8,000-square-foot gallery comprising of a floor-to-ceiling wooden ark, fun interactive play, crawl-through tunnels, climbing nets, pretend play areas, and a whimsical animal puppet show, this experience captures the spirit of play, curiosity, and wonder in a tangible way. Not only is it beautifully designed with high-quality and upcycled materials, it immediately transports you into a world of whimsical wonder with much humor.

Medium: Immersive Children's Playground
Action: Discover, Interact, and Play

Spyscape HQ (New York City)

In addition to serving as a museum of everything espionage, Spyscape HQ gives visitors a chance to step into the shoes of becoming a spy. By exploring their skills in immersive challenges such as lie detection, codebreaking, and

---

[40] https://www.skirball.org/noahs-ark

laser tunnels, visitors also get the opportunity to discover their own attributes and potential as a spy. This experience is modern, sleek, and highly engaging for all ages.

Medium: Interactive Museum
Action: Discover and Interact

The Nest (Los Angeles, California)

In *The Nest,* up to two visitors at a time enter an intimate, packed storage unit with multiple themed spaces that capture a woman's life in objects. Using tape recorders, projectors, and other found objects, visitors explore and discover each chapter of her story in a visceral and intuitive way. This experience beautifully captures a literal walk-through of someone's life, revealing engaging layers of emotional storytelling. (Please see color photo section.)

Medium: Interactive and Immersive Experience
Action: Explore, Discover, and Interact

teamLab Planets TOKYO (Toyosu, Tokyo, Japan)

teamLab Planets is a museum where visitors walk through water and explore a garden where they "become one with the flowers." In four massive exhibition spaces and two gardens, visitors enter barefoot and immerse their entire bodies with other people in the immersive artworks. The boundaries between the self, others, the artwork, and the world dissolve and become continuous, as visitors explore a new relationship without boundaries.

From the immersive artwork *Floating Flower Garden* consisting of a three-dimensional mass of flowers that rises when people are near it, to *Drawing on the Water Surface Created by the Dance of Koi and People - Infinity*, featuring Koi whose trajectories are determined by the presence of people, the experience creates a sense of play, wonder, and imaginative co-creation.

Medium: Interactive and Immersive Digital Art Installation
Action: Explore, Discover, Immerse, Interact, Play, and Create
(Please see the color photo section.)

BRAINSTORMING THE MEDIUM AND AUDIENCE ACTION

The medium supports the action of the audience in a way that embraces the theme and wish fulfillment. Consider all of the options, and determine which medium best celebrates your story and transforms your audience. You may brainstorm a few ideas and capture them on notecards (digital or paper). Also remember that the audience action can include more than just sight and sound. It can also include taste, touch, and smell.

You can add as many (or as few) categories as you want on your notecard to help visualize and organize your ideas. Let's take the classic story of Lewis Carroll's *Alice in Wonderland* and brainstorm an interpretation of his story into an experience.

Story: Interpretation of Lewis Carroll's *Alice in Wonderland*

Why Tell This Story: To remind us of the glorious days of childhood.

Theme: Growing up as a child in an adult world is scary and confusing.

Where is the Authenticity: Personalities (Meet the beloved characters)

Wish Fulfillment: Experience a child-like view of the world (everything is in a giant scale), the garden party with White Rabbit, encounter iconic characters from story, go on an adventure with the characters.

Medium: Immersive, multi-sensory, walkthrough experience

Action: Walk, dine, character encounter

Action Details: Follow the White Rabbit into a hole under a tree, drink a potion and enter a door, come out the other side to Wonderland. Attend a garden party with the Rabbit and your group (scones and tea included). Encounter characters like the Red Queen and Tweedledee and Tweedledum.

Transformation/Change in Audience: Never forget the innocence and curiosity of your youth.

WHAT IS THE ROLE OF
YOUR AUDIENCE?

Next comes the definition of your audience's role in the story. Notice how the audience comes before the characters in your experience. The visitor experience is always the priority. They are there to fulfill their fantasy, so you need to ensure that their role is compelling and engaging.

Here's my take on the six types of audience roles:

1) Visitor

2) Spectator

3) Participant — Immersive

4) Participant — Interactive

5) Hero

6) Creator

THE VISITOR

Many experiences are indifferent to the visitor, meaning that the design of the story and experience remains unchanged regardless of who or how many visitors are present. Art galleries, museum exhibits, art installations, playgrounds — these are all examples of places for "visitors." The experience is not immersive, and is designed for any type of visitor to come and go based on normal operating hours. Employees of the experience (if there are any) are not part of the story, rather, they work for the establishment that hosts the experience.

THE SPECTATOR

A spectator is acknowledged, but does not participate in the show or experience. Some examples are sporting events, concerts, dance performances, theater shows, and immersive themed dining. There is a clear delineation between the spectators and the athletes/performers/staff members. The spectators are acknowledged as guests and are occasionally prompted to cheer and respond. The spectator's participation does not directly influence the outcome of the story or experience.

A terrific example of a spectator experience is the *Space 220 Restaurant*[41] in EPCOT at Walt Disney World (Orlando, Florida). Upon arrival, you enter a "space elevator" that transports you to a restaurant located 220 miles above the planet. Breathtaking panoramic views of space immerse diners in a celestial environment, giving them the unique opportunity to dine among the stars.

PARTICIPANT – IMMERSIVE

A participant in an immersive experience can freely explore and discover a themed environment without directly interacting with the story. Punchdrunk's *Sleep No More* is an example in which the audience can freely roam about as observers and voyeurs to the story, but the experience continues without requiring audience interaction. They are, for the most part, "invisible" to the cast of characters. (Unless, of course, you are one of the lucky few

---

[41] https://disneyworld.disney.go.com/dining/epcot/space-220/

who get pulled into an intimate experience with one of the performers.)

Another example of an immersive experience for a participant is Meow Wolf's *House of Eternal Return*. Participants can explore a completely immersive environment, but do not interact with characters or influence the story. They are immersed in a rich world and can discover hidden details and story elements, but cannot change their surroundings based on their actions. There are some basic interactive elements to the experience, but overall, the experience can be enjoyed without any interactivity.

PARTICIPANT - INTERACTIVE

A participant in an interactive experience can interact with the story and characters in engaging ways that don't influence the structure or outcome of the experience. The participant's interactive action, however, is *key* to the experience design. The experience cannot be fully enjoyed and realized without audience interactivity.

Rides that offer interactive play are examples of interactive experiences. *Buzz Lightyear Astro Blasters*, found in multiple Disney theme parks, is an evolution of a carnival game, where the audience blasts alien targets while riding on a vehicle with the goal of achieving a high score.

Just Fix It Productions' *The Willows*[42] is a more extreme example of an interactive experience in which the participant can interact with the story and characters. They describe the experience on their website as "a combination

---

[42] https://www.jfiproductions.com/the-willows

of interactive and site-specific theatre, providing an exhilarating evening full of exploration and discovery."

I experienced this little gem a few years ago as one of eighteen visitors "invited to a dinner by the Willows" inside a 10,000 square-foot mansion in the greater Los Angeles area. During this two-hour "modern-day psychological mystery" experience, I discovered a dark secret while engaging with the cast of characters in various activities, including a sit-down dinner, a slow dance, and card games. I was taken to the bathroom for an intimate moment with a character who brushed my hair and told me to lie down in a bathtub as she told me the story of how her brother died. What a creepy, but unique experience! The company has since developed an interactive VR feature film based on this experience.

HERO

The hero experience is the future of immersive storytelling. Consider video games in which you play a character on a mission. How you perform and react to situations determines the outcome of the game experience. In gaming, there are so many examples of linear and multilinear (branching) storytelling in which your actions determine your fate.

In themed experiences, we have only just begun to explore the possibilities of the audience as the "hero." We have seen examples of the audience as "hero" in escape rooms and in live action role-playing, also known as LARP, a type of interactive and immersive role-playing game in which the participants portray characters through physical action. Characters are often dressed in costumes and props, and engage in immersive environments where they perform missions, play games, participate in events, or simply immerse themselves in a world that responds to their actions.

Examples of such places include Evermore Park[43] in Pleasant Grove, Utah, where participants are encouraged to dress up with props, find unique names for themselves, and enter as "world walkers" to a strange land. They enter the "portal of an ancient, mystical world" where warriors, royalty, elves, goblins, dragons reside. The visitors embark on quests, interact with characters, join guilds, watch performances, and participate in activities like archery and axe-throwing.

In the multi-day adventure *Star Wars: Galactic Starcruiser*[44] at Walt Disney World Resort, "passengers" sleep, dine, and play in the immersive world of *Star Wars*. Participants interact with characters and follow different storylines, depending on their chosen affiliations.

CREATOR

Last, but not least, the creator experience promises that the visitor can fully determine their story based on their desired action and wish fulfillment. We see examples of this in video games such as *Minecraft* where players can create their own environments without any set objectives or outcomes. It truly is an opportunity for players to unleash their inner creativity and express their imagination within the set parameters of the world.

---

[43] https://www.evermore.com
[44] https://disneyworld.disney.go.com/star-wars-galactic-starcruiser/

I look forward to seeing what a creator experience will be like in theme parks and other formats of immersive storytelling. How can you create a "sandbox" with unlimited resources and opportunities for your guests? And how can that experience be enjoyed by other participants' engagement? How do the worlds they create manifest into a design that is compelling, holistic, and meaningful?

The design of your experience will determine the role of your audience. Do you want them to have agency and explore the world and have influence on the experience to determine the outcome of the story? Or do you simply want your audience to be immersed in your world?

Depending on the audience action and the different levels of engagement, you may want to consider different options before committing. Remember, the more agency you give to your audience, the more you have to ensure that the story fulfills on the promise of the experience (since you will have less control over the beginning, middle, and end of each participant's story). This is where you have to lean in on emotional anchors to your experience, where each unique space, activity, ride, or show has an emotional and thematic tie-in to the experience.

Audience Verbs

Another way to develop and further define the six types of audience roles is to consider the audience's actions with verbs. In other words, what are the actions that your audience will partake in your experience? Use verbs to outline your audience's role.

1) **Visitor**
   o Verbs: Discover, Learn, Play, Question

2) **Spectator**
   o Verbs: Watch, Observe

3) **Participant — Immersive**
   o Verbs: Explore, Discover, Engage, Share

4) **Participant — Interactive**
   o Verbs: Dine, Drink, Drive, Target, Push, Pull, Play, Smell, Touch, Crawl

5) **Hero**
   o Verbs: Dress up, Roleplay, Dine, Play, Become, Transform

6) **Creator**
   o Verbs: Create, Deconstruct, Invite, Collaborate

By considering the verbs for your audience's role, you ensure that their role is vital to the experience. They are not mere spectators if they are jumping, pushing, playing, interacting, and talking. Depending on the kind of experience you're designing, you should always consider the possibilities (which also helps to set the parameters for the audience participation, which I'll discuss in a later chapter). What can your audience do in your experience that will not only meet, but exceed, their expectations? Exceeding your audience's expectations means having them walk away saying, "I didn't expect to enjoy that. In fact, I loved it."

If you're designing to a status quo without having any aspirations of changing the status quo, then your experience will fall flat. How can you put a spin on your audience's expectations for the format that you're offering?

Derek DelGaudio's "In & Of Itself" (New York City)

Illusionist Derek DelGaudio's theatrical performance *In & Of Itself*[45], originally ran off Broadway in NYC for 500 performances before airing on Hulu as a documentary. DelGaudio attempts to understand the illusory nature of identity and answer the deceptively simple question "Who am I?"

Derek's show defied the traditional understanding of a "theater show." Rather than have his audience merely sitting and watching a performance, Derek broke through the barrier between performer and spectator, and seamlessly and brilliantly wove the audience into the fabric of the narrative.

When audience members first walked into the show venue, they were asked to select a title card off a wall that defined their identity. Words like "Teacher," "Mother," "Oracle," or "Rebel." He asked the audience to take a moment and consider how they self-identified. DelGaudio realized that if he wanted to transform the audience, he would have to invite the audience to get in touch with their own identities and stories.

During the show, Derek performed sleight-of-hand card tricks and other magical performances that met the audience's expectations of what defined a "magic show." However, towards the end of the show, he approached each audience member, looked deeply into their eyes,

---

[45] https://www.inandofitselfshow.com

and somehow identified what title card each of them had chosen at the start of the show. This act of "seeing his audience" was so moving that it moved many of the audience members to tears.

Derek and his audience became integral characters in his story, interwoven and transformed by the end of the performance. He took it even a step further by having one audience member leave and return to a separate night's performance in order to continue the narrative.

The audience couldn't help but feel that they were part of a bigger narrative, a bigger universe in which each one of them played an important role — that we are not important only in our own lives, but in each other's lives as well. We are all so interwoven that we can't exist individually. That our stories start, end, and continue with one another.

WHAT ARE THE RULES OF ENGAGEMENT?

Once you've defined your audience role, you want to explore your audience's rules of engagement, also called the "pre-engagement" experience. These parameters set your audience's expectations for *how* to engage.

You've created a world/exhibit/experience, but like any interaction, there are limits. Setting up the expectations beforehand is a sure way for your audience to understand the "rules." Yes, your audience is supposed to have fun and engage with your experience in surprising and unimaginable ways, but setting the rules and parameters ensures that one visitor can enjoy it as much as any other visitor. These rules can come in the form of FAQs on a website or e-mail, in-story communication with your audience prior to the experience, or right before the experience in the form of media or a live host.

Rules and parameters are especially important if you're designing an experience that has never been done before. If you're creating a completely new story paradigm, then your audience must quickly and easily understand how to "play" in a safe and enjoyable manner. After all, they are committing their time and money to your experience. You want to set parameters for them to understand how best to safely enjoy your experience. Bonus points for writing them in-story!

For example, prior to arriving for *The Nest* experience, visitors receive an e-mail detailing the arrival instructions, as well as other warnings and considerations. *The Nest* clearly states that in the 60–75-minute experience, visitors will "walk, duck, navigate small spaces, stand for periods of time, and be in moments of complete darkness." Attached to the e-mail, there's an in-story explanation of WHY you're coming to the experience — you've won an auction for a storage unit previously owned by a Josephine Carroll, who passed away a few months ago. Sending an e-mail with real world instructions, but adding the attached in-story memo from the auction house, is a clever way to pre-engage with your audience and create anticipation.

Consider how you can share the rules of your experience in a fun and engaging manner. Create intrigue for your audience, but set realistic expectations. Often times, this form of communication is the first thing your audience engages with. Put your best foot forward and wow your audience. Like a movie trailer, your rules of engagement set the story before your audience has the opportunity to experience it. It's the teaser before the main attraction.

WHAT ARE THE EMOTIONAL ANCHORS OF YOUR EXPERIENCE?

Why is it important to have emotional anchors? Creating emotional anchors will increase the likelihood that each member of your audience will have the same emotional takeaway relating to the theme and wish fulfillment of your experience. This ties directly to my earlier point of identifying the core "feeling" of your experience. If you're familiar with screenwriting for TV and film, think of the emotional anchors as the major plot points to your story. They are the "can't miss" moments that define your story. They're the walk on Main Street, U.S.A. to Sleeping Beauty's Castle and the fireworks at the end of the day in Disneyland. They're the emotional anchors that bookend and highlight your journey from beginning to end.

These emotional anchors or "plot points" keep the story moving forward in an emotionally engaging way. They keep the audience's interest to discover and explore further. Like a movie or TV script, it propels the story forward, but unlike a movie or TV script, the protagonist is your audience. Your audience will choose what they want to experience next, so building these emotional anchors are vital to your experience.

Some ideas on how to create emotional "anchors" to your experience:

1) **Bookend your experience with shows or scenes that your audience must attend.**

   o At the start of the immersive theatrical experience, *Sleep No More*, the audience is encouraged to enjoy drinks at the bar before they are greeted by one of the actors. They are instructed to don white masks during the three-hour experience and are given a set of rules and a closing remark that "fortune favors the bold."

   o At the end of the *Sleep No More* experience, all participants are gathered by the actors to the banquet room where the final act takes place on stage.

2) **Diversify your experience with various emotional tones**

   o Embrace emotional tones that tie to the theme of the experience. In *Star Wars: Galaxy's Edge*, we created rides, shops, dining establishments, and other locations that represented the different emotional tones of *Star Wars*. (Please see color photo section.)

   o *Savi's Workshop — Handbuilt Lightsabers*[46] was the "heart" of the land. This is where we heavily leaned into the Force and the theme of the entire land which was that "your choices have consequences." The emotional tone was that of intimacy and belonging. Here, those strong in the Force have gathered to build their unique lightsaber.

---

[46] https://disneyworld.disney.go.com/shops/hollywood-studios/savis-workshop-handbuilt-lightsabers/

o In *Star Wars: Rise of the Resistance*[47], we leaned into the emotional tone of thrilling heroism. Like many scenes in *Star Wars* where the Resistance are battling with the First Order, we wanted to capture that feeling by placing the visitors in the middle of an epic climactic battle.

o In *Oga's Cantina*[48], we wanted to capture the emotional tone of joy and celebration. This is the place for all *Star Wars* fans to gather and geek out about all things they love about *Star Wars*. Names of the drinks, fun drink coasters, songs played by DJ R-3X, the creatures found in the bar counter, even training Cast Members to hit on the hyperdrive engine and encouraging everyone to sing "Yocola Ateema," which translates to "drink now" in the Huttese language (one of the many species languages of *Star Wars*). This is the place to party and celebrate. Our cantina is our love letter to *Star Wars*.

o In *Millennium Falcon: Smugglers Run*,[49] we captured the wish fulfillment of becoming a smuggler by embracing the emotional tone of friendship and comradery as visitors work as a crew to perform an important mission. This experience is all about teamwork. The stronger your crew communicates with one another, the better your chances of succeeding in the mission.

---

[47] https://disneyworld.disney.go.com/attractions/hollywood-studios/star-wars-rise-of-the-resistance/
[48] https://disneyworld.disney.go.com/dining/hollywood-studios/ogas-cantina/
[49] https://disneyworld.disney.go.com/attractions/hollywood-studios/millennium-falcon-smugglers-run/

Market entrance at *Star Wars: Galaxy's Edge* in Disneyland. Photo: Margaret Kerrison.

o In the *Black Spire Outpost Market*, we embraced the emotional tones of awe, surprise, and nostalgia. All of the shops and dining locales are representative of the various things we love from *Star Wars*. From Jedi and Sith robes to creatures to toys/games, we made sure that all eras of *Star Wars* were represented.

3) Populate your experience with beloved characters

o Never underestimate the power of characters. By bringing characters into your experience (whether they are original or pre-existing), they signal to your audience what they should be feeling and how they should be reacting to the world around them.

o Characters are a great way for children, as well as an international, multi-generational audiences, to engage with your story.

Costume photo op, Peranakan Museum, Singapore. Photo: Foster Kerrison

teamLab, *Floating Flower Garden: Flowers and I are of the Same Root, the Garden and I are One*, 2015, Interactive Kinetic Installation, Endless, Sound: Hideaki Takahashi © teamLab, courtesy Pace Gallery

teamLab, *Drawing on the Water Surface Created by the Dance of Koi and People - Infinity*, 2016-2018, Interactive Digital Installation, Endless, Sound: Hideaki Takahashi © teamLab, courtesy Pace Gallery

teamLab, *Moss Garden of Resonating Microcosms - Solidified Light Color, Sunrise and Sunset*, 2021, Interactive Digital Installation, Endless, Sound: Hideaki Takahashi © teamLab, courtesy Pace Gallery

Meow Wolf's *House of Eternal Return*, Santa Fe, New Mexico. Photo: Kate Russell. Courtesy of Meow Wolf.

Meow Wolf's *House of Eternal Return*, Santa Fe, New Mexico. Photo: Kate Russell. Courtesy of Meow Wolf.

Meow Wolf's *Omega Mart* Las Vegas. Photo: Kate Russell. Courtesy of Meow Wolf.

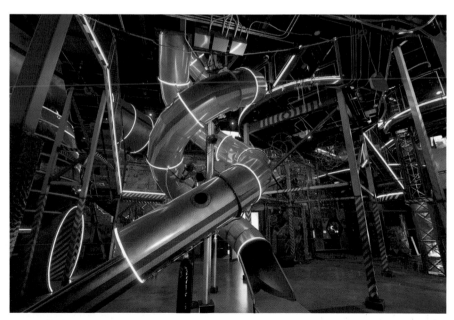

Meow Wolf's *Omega Mart* Las Vegas. Photo: Kate Russell. Courtesy of Meow Wolf.

Lost Spirits Distillery Las Vegas. Photo: Wonho Frank Lee

Lost Spirits Distillery Las Vegas. Photo: Wonho Frank Lee

Lost Spirits Distillery Las Vegas. Photo: Randy Phommahaxay

The Speakeasy San Francisco.
Photo: Peter Liu

Sleep No More at The
McKittrick Hotel. Photo:
Robin Roemer

The Nest Los Angeles. Photo:
Jeremey Connors

SPYSCAPE New York City. Courtesy of SPYSCAPE

NASA Kennedy Space Center Visitor Complex, Merritt Island, Florida. Photo: Margaret Kerrison

Underwood Family Farms, Moorpark, CA, Photo: Margaret Kerrison

Cars Land, Disney California Adventure

The Wizarding World of Harry Potter™ at Universal Orlando. Photo: Aditya Vyas for Unsplash

The Wizarding World of Harry Potter™ at Universal Orlando. Photo: Brian McGowan for Unsplash

The Wizarding World of Harry Potter™ at Universal Orlando. Photo: Aditya Vyas for Unsplash

Star Wars: Galaxy's Edge in Disneyland, California. Photo: Margaret Kerrison

Star Wars: Galaxy's Edge in Disneyland, California. Photo: Rod Long for Unsplash

Star Wars: Galaxy's Edge in Disneyland, California. Photo: Rod Long for Unsplash

Star Wars: Galaxy's Edge in Disneyland, California. Photo: Rod Long for Unsplash

Star Wars: Galaxy's Edge in Disneyland, California. Photo: Margaret Kerrison

Star Wars: Galaxy's Edge in Disneyland, California. Photo: Becky Fantham for Unsplash

o Characters don't necessarily have to be walkaround characters. They can appear in the form of visual media, audio, puppets, robotics, props, or graphics.

o Introduce a villain/antagonist to your story and your audience will experience emotions of fear, anger, horror and/or disgust.

o Introduce a hero/protagonist to your story and your audience will experience emotions of admiration, adoration, awe, excitement, interest, triumph, and/or pride.

4) Focus on universal truths and emotions

o It's so tempting to keep up with trends and do "what the kids are saying and doing these days." If your experience is going to last for a short amount of time, I say go for it, if it's aligned with the theme. Keep in mind, however, that trends come and go. Your experience may become outdated in no time, if your focus is "trying to keep up with the kids." If you're developing a permanent installation, don't fall for trends. Keep it classic and evergreen. Stick with universal human truths and emotions. You can't go wrong with elements that will never change no matter what's going on in the world.

You can choose to use one or more of these ideas to bring emotional anchors to your experience. Ultimately, you want to identify enough emotional anchors to ensure that the promise of your story is intact and that the theme and wish fulfillment meet your audience's expectations.

WHO ARE THE CHARACTERS IN YOUR STORY?

In the previous chapter, we discussed the importance of creating emotional anchors to your experience. There is no better way to create emotion than to introduce compelling characters in your story. The characters that you meet in your experience represent the cast of your world, and it should be more than just the hero and villain.

Supporting characters are just as important as your main characters. They reveal different sides of your main characters' lives that your audience can relate to or identify with. They also create a deeper, richer sense of your world in ways that can be surprising and revealing to your audience. They also support the main character's story arc.

One of my favorite writers, Margaret Atwood, explains in her MasterClass that

> A well-written supporting character will have a character arc, a strong point of view, and clear personality traits. In many cases they will be the types of characters a reader might recognize from their own life and — like main characters — they will grow and change over the course of the storyline. Characters who don't change are known as flat characters, and while certain bit parts work just fine as flat characters, the majority of your secondary parts must be dynamic and engaging to a reader or viewer.[50]

---

[50] https://www.masterclass.com/articles/how-to-write-supporting-characters#margaret-atwoods-8-tips-for-writing-supporting-characters

Whether it's from an existing story in which you have to choose which characters you'd like your audience to meet or characters that you have to create for an original story, these characters should be diverse and representative of your target audience's wish fulfillment. In other words, which characters would fulfill your audience's fantasy of experiencing your story?

There are many different character archetypes that you can choose from. The term "archetype" means *original pattern* in ancient Greek. The Swiss psychiatrist and psychoanalyst Carl Jung, the founder of analytical psychology, built his theory of the human psyche on the concept of archetypes. He described twelve universal character archetypes that are shaped in our collective unconscious.[51] We often use these archetypes in storytelling.

Jung's Twelve Character Archetypes
- Ruler
- Creator/Artist
- Sage
- Innocent
- Explorer
- Rebel
- Hero
- Wizard
- Jester
- Everyman
- Lover
- Caregiver

---

[51] https://conorneill.com/2018/04/21/understanding-personality-the-12-jungian-archetypes/

Christopher Vogler, in his book *The Writer's Journey*[52], draws on material from Joseph Campbell's *The Hero with a Thousand Faces*, to compile a list of eight character archetypes in the hero's journey. These character types include: the hero, mentor, ally, herald, trickster, shapeshifter, guardian, and shadow.

- Hero — The protagonist; the central character to the story. We root for the success of the hero.
- Mentor — The one who gives the hero advice and wisdom in order to complete their journey.
- Ally — Supports the hero in their journey through companionship, knowledge, and general help.
- Herald — A character, object, or event that propels the hero in their journey.
- Trickster — Brings humor to the story, but can also serve as someone who challenges the status quo and makes the hero think differently.
- Shapeshifter — The character who changes from the first time we meet them in the story to someone who may help or hinder the hero's journey.
- Guardian — A character or object that prevents an obstacle to the hero's journey.
- Shadow — The antagonist is a character or event that serves as the largest obstacle to prevent the hero from getting what they want. This can be a villain, a group of invading aliens, or a natural disaster like a hurricane.

Creating a diversity of character archetypes in your story creates a richer, more fascinating world. Consider the

---

[52] Christopher Vogler, *The Writer's Journey: Mythic Structure for Writers*, 25th Anniversary (Fourth) edition (Studio City, CA: Michael Wiese Productions, 2007, 2020) pp. 3-4, 25-27.

Game of Thrones books by George R.R. Martin and the television series that they inspired. Martin constructs a world chockfull of interesting characters with different backgrounds, all vying for the same thing — to sit on the Iron Throne and rule all of the kingdoms. He skillfully creates different archetypes that each of us can identify with and root for.

Which of these character archetypes can help support and strengthen your experience? What form will they take? As I mentioned in the previous chapter, they don't necessarily have to be living, breathing, walkaround characters. They can appear in the form of visual media, audio, puppets, robotics, props, or graphics. Mix it up and use a combination of these media to represent the diverse cast of characters in your story.

Wizarding World of Harry Potter

You can't have a *Wizarding World of Harry Potter*[53] without meeting Harry Potter and his friends Hermione Granger and Ron Weasley. In addition to these main characters, you will need to add more characters that represent the enormous, wonderful cast from J.K. Rowling's books. Which will you choose?

It comes back to the wish fulfillment. We discussed that in this world, you would want to visit Hogwarts Castle and go to Ollivander's. At Hogwarts Castle, you would want to meet Harry's best friends, Hermione and Ron, as well as the professors and other important supporting characters that portray this rich world, such as the animated portraits

---

[53] https://www.universalorlando.com/web/en/us/universal-orlando-resort/the-wizarding-world-of-harry-potter/hub

that appear on the walls of Hogwarts. There are so many characters to choose from, but which are the characters that are integral to Harry Potter's story? Professors like Albus Dumbledore, Minerva McGonagall, Remus Lupin, Rubeus Hagrid, and who can forget, Severus Snape, are all recurring characters that you definitely want to meet at Hogwarts.

In the book, Harry met with Garrick Ollivander himself when he received his wand. In a theme park setting, however, you may not be able to guarantee a particular character for every visitor experience. You want to diversify the talent pool so that you can hire top quality performers who can deliver on the promise of the experience. How do you construct a story that explains why you're meeting with other people, rather than Ollivander? By having the audience meet with employees of Ollivander's Wand Shop, the audience can experience "the wish fulfillment moment" of having the wand choose you in a fun and surprising retail experience. Then you can employ a diverse cast, which includes people of varying ages.

A CAST OF ORIGINAL CHARACTERS

What happens when you're creating an original story and your characters aren't pre-determined? The same rule applies: Create characters that would fulfill your audience's fantasy of your story. What's the promise of the experience?

Dreamscape Immersive's Alien Zoo

In this virtual reality experience, Dreamscape Immersive had to create a world and story that was appropriate for the medium to fulfill the fantasy of exploring an alien landscape. The title of the experience says it all — the promise is that you're going to an "alien zoo." Therefore, the "characters" you would expect to meet are alien wild-life creatures.

The audience invitation is to "take a breathtaking tour of a wildlife refuge in space" where they can meet an "astounding assortment of lifeforms from the far corners of the universe"[54] collected all in one place to save them from extinction. That's a pretty straightforward story that delivers on the promise of the experience.

DIVERSITY AND REPRESENTATION

In thinking about your cast of characters, it is important to embrace diversity and representation. Remember that your experience should be welcoming to all audiences, even though you have a target audience in mind. In creating your characters, you want to challenge what has been done before, defy stereotypes, and redefine gender roles that are relevant to our times.

As a writer who considers herself to be multicultural, I've never felt comfortable ticking just one box to define who I am. I was born in Indonesia as a Chinese ethnic minority, but moved to Singapore when I was four years old to attend an American school. I spoke a mixture of Bahasa Indonesia and Javanese at home with my parents and relatives, but spoke English to my siblings and friends.

---

[54] https://dreamscapeimmersive.com/adventures/details/alienzoo01

We are all complicated human beings with vast experiences, histories, and backgrounds. You want your experience to be representative and inclusive of your audience. If they don't "see" themselves in the experience or feel that they haven't been "invited to the party," then they are less likely to be engaged or emotionally invested.

Fellow Imagineer Dave Durham shared the story of when he and his family visited the *Adventure Thru Inner Space* attraction for the first time in the 1970s. As a young Black boy, he was horrified at what he saw in the queue where the show prop "ride vehicles" went into one end of a tube and came out miniaturized. The miniaturization wasn't the traumatic part for Dave. It was the idea that everyone in the ride vehicles turned into white people, as demonstrated in the show's moving prop of everyone coming out of the other end of the tube as mini white figures sitting in the ride vehicles. He cowered and told his family, "That machine turns you white!"

Consider that in a few decades, the demographic makeup of the United States is going to change drastically. Your audience today may change sooner than you think. According to Pew Research Center, a majority of the U.S. population will be nonwhite by the year 2050.[55] Blacks, Hispanics, Asians, and other minorities will constitute a majority of the population. Furthermore, according to the U.S. Census Bureau, by the year 2050, people who are 65 and older will outnumber those younger than 18.

In developing characters, you want to consider other factors that represent a diverse audience. Create characters

---

[55] www.pewsocialtrends.org/2019/03/21/views-of-demographic-changes-in-america/

that are believable and aspirational so that they may leave a positive impression on your audience. Represent characters with different abilities and disabilities, body aesthetics, shapes, sizes, cultures, and languages. Is your hero in a wheelchair? Does she have a speech impediment? Does your character wear glasses like Harry Potter? A hijab? Do all of your characters need to be good-looking? Can they be younger? Older? Can they come from different socio-economic backgrounds? Do they speak in different languages? Do they communicate in sign language? Go against stereotypes. The hero doesn't have to be the good-looking blonde or brunette. Can the love story occur between two people of the same gender? Does the mechanic have to be a man?

Don't make a character a person of color just to include diversity and stop your work there. Be sure that your minority character depicts a fully-formed character and avoid stereotypes and generalizations. Receive feedback from different people, especially the group that you're representing. The last thing you want to do is create a character formed by your own unconscious biases.

As a writer, you have the power to imagine a world others cannot experience in their daily lives. When people see themselves in your stories, they will feel more connected to your world. Do your homework and conduct some research. Then get honest feedback and peer reviews from the appropriate people. Depict a world you want to live in. Bring unity and positivity in your messaging.

Remember, by telling a story that embraces emotions and universal truths, your story can be timeless. Remind yourself that a story is told from the creator's perspective, so it can influence and impact entire generations. As a storyteller, you have the power and responsibility to bring hope, joy, and optimism to the world. You have the power to influence and inspire minds. Use the power of your words to represent an authentic, diverse, and inclusive world. You owe it to future generations.

CHARACTER CHART

Depending on the scope of your project, you may want to develop a character chart to include all of the different characters in your story and their relationships with one another. You may include a brief description for each of the characters, so that the chart becomes more of a quick visual tool, rather than something comprehensive like a character treatment or bible.

Here's a sample template of a character chart that you can use in developing your characters. You can add as many rows and columns as you'd like, but the goal is to keep it concise, so it's easy to read and comprehend.

NAME/ IMAGE	AGE	GENDER	RACE/ SPECIES	BIRTH- PLACE	IDEOLOGY/ BELIEFS	BACK- STORY	RELATION- SHIPS

WHERE IS YOUR STORY SET?

In a previous chapter, we used the example of *Alice in Wonderland* to brainstorm the medium of the experience and the action of the audience, but what if the setting for your story is not as clear? What if you're creating an original story that doesn't have a pre-existing setting or world for your experience?

Don't fret. Like any good story, there's always an ideal setting. By looking at all of the factors that you've gathered thus far, you can start to visualize your ideal setting.

Consider all of the factors we have discussed thus far:

Why Tell This Story
Target Audience
Audience Feeling
Change in Audience
Theme
Authenticity
Wish Fulfillment
Tone/Mood
Medium
Action
Audience Role
Emotional Anchors
Characters

In a step-by-step approach, try to fill out the list as best as you can in a few words. Depending on who the characters are, we can determine where your audience will meet them. Furthermore, using your theme, wish fulfillment, and tone/mood, you can better visualize where you would like your audience to meet your characters.

Let's take a hypothetical example of a client hiring you to develop an exhibit about the importance of nature and our role to protect it. They want a setting where they can educate the public about the significant human impact on nature.

Let's try to fill out the list with this information from the perspective of the Audience.

Why Tell This Story — We need to do everything we can to protect nature.

Target Audience — All ages

Audience Feeling — I love nature. Nature is important to me and everyone around me.

Change in Audience — How can I change my daily habits to protect and conserve this world for myself and future generations? What can I do?

Theme — We protect what we love.

Authenticity — The value of nature

Wish Fulfillment — I want to enjoy nature and enjoy it with my loved ones.

Tone/Mood — Hopeful, curious, surprising

Medium — Small group eco-tour

Action — Explore the wonders of nature and understand the effects that we have on the environment.

Audience Role — Participatory- Immersive

Emotional Anchors — Bookends — Introductory pre-show to answer the question of "Why tell this story?" End the experience with an inspirational experience to make me understand what changes I can make today to protect nature and better the environment.

Characters — Meet "characters" in the form of locals, naturalists, and environmental experts (in-person, media, and graphics).

In looking at all of the factors, it's becoming obvious that in order to tell a story about the importance of nature, the most effective way to create a change in the audience is to place them *in nature*. As much as a museum exhibit would be a viable option, why not create an immersive experience in which the audience can have a multisensory experience? You can consider offering both options. You can start with the museum exhibit and have the premium experience of being immersed in nature, in the form of an eco-tour.

An eco-tour can come in many forms. It can be a guided trek experience through a forest or jungle with some participatory elements, such as observations and discussions of the natural setting in question. If an in-person trek through a forest or jungle is not practical, then can the tour be conducted from a jeep or car? If you want your audience to fall in love with something, then you have to bring them face-to-face with the thing you want them to fall in love with, in this case, the natural setting itself.

By placing your audience in an ideal setting, you are one step closer to creating an emotionally compelling experience that ties to the theme and wish fulfillment of your project.

MULTIPLE LOCATIONS IN A SETTING

Within your setting, you may decide to have multiple locations, depending on the scale of your project. Each of those locations should have a separate location name, theme, story, environment, emotion/feeling, character(s), and staff role.

Below is an example of a location story chart that breaks down each location per category. By filling out each of the columns, you'll get a better sense of each location and why it's important to your larger story. All of the locations should be connected to each other and support the greater theme.

LOCATION	THEME	STORY	SETTING	EMOTION	CHARACTERS	STAFF ROLE
What is it and why is it here?	What is the theme?	What is happening?	What does it look like?	What does it feel like?	Who do you meet?	How does the staff fit into the story?

You can decide to add more rows and columns depending on the scope of your project. It becomes a useful tool, especially for the wider team, to get a "snapshot" view of each location and its story without having to read the entire character's backstory.

A NOTE ABOUT CULTURAL APPROPRIATION IN SETTINGS

There is nothing wrong with being inspired by different cultures and countries, but be careful not to claim that you are making an authentic representation of a people, city, or country without receiving the feedback and support from the group/culture you're trying to represent. Remember that you are telling a story through your unique eyes, and there's a good chance that your unconscious bias will find its way to your setting. What you see as "exotic" may be very different from someone who comes from that culture or country. What you choose to highlight in your environment may not be one that the people from the country would choose.

Do your part. Always bring in the appropriate experts and people to your project to ensure that the setting you're creating is not misusing or misrepresenting a people or culture. You have to invest in your research and education to deeply understand and appreciate a culture before attempting to represent it in any way.

What can you do to avoid cultural appropriation? Here are some suggestions.

- Do your research from credible and reliable sources.
- Bring in experts and members of the culture who authentically represent the group and culture. Take the time to listen to their stories and ideas.

- Visit the authentic locations and take the time to learn, understand, and appreciate the culture.
- Give credit or recognize the culture you are learning from. Do not claim it as your own.
- Collaborate and provide opportunities for members of the culture to work on your project, sell their goods/ services, and contribute in a way that's meaningful to them.

WHEN DOES YOUR
STORY TAKE PLACE?

In considering your setting, you may consider a different timeline. Does your story occur in the past, present, or future? Maybe the story occurs in an alternate timeline of the past, present, or future. *When* your story takes place informs you as the storyteller and ultimately, the designers, about the elements to include (and exclude) in the placemaking.

The time period creates a believable world for the characters and your visitors to pursue their fantasies. It also sets the promise and expectation of what your visitors will experience.

For example, Secret Cinema & Fever's *Bridgerton* experience promises a three-hour soirée for guests to get a taste of life among 1813 English high society as they step into the delightful (yet scandalous) world of the Netflix original series *Bridgerton.*[56]

The experience promises to fulfill every guest's fantasy of attending "The Ball of The Season" in a secret London location. Your hostess? Lady Whistledown. In this time period, you would fully expect a grand ballroom filled with fancy gowns and tailcoats, but also a gentlemen's duel,

---

[56] https://secretbridgertonball.com

waltzing and dance cards, among other unique 19th century affairs.

Consider the when of your experience to create an immersive environment in which your guests can fully and willingly escape reality and transport themselves into a time period of their wildest fantasy.

It's one thing to create a temporary, limited-time experience, but what if you're designing an experience that will be installed in a more permanent format? Keep in mind the longevity and flexibility of your time period. Will it still feel compelling one year, five years, ten years from today? Will there be new storylines that will conflict with your current storyline? You should always plan for flexibility in your design so that new characters and storylines can enter your world without creating confusion for your visitors.

WHAT ARE THE COMPARABLES?

In designing any experience, it's important to understand the comparables and competitors from a creative
perspective. In the industry, we would go on "benchmark-
ing trips." We would visit different locations to learn, be
inspired, and understand what we would do differently.
Often times, we travel as a team so we can experience it
together and have opportunities to discuss the locations.

Consider what experiences have characteristics that are
similar to your project. What experiences are direct competitors? What works and what doesn't? How can you
improve upon the experience? What makes your experience unique from others? How can you make your
experience stand out?

Here are some suggestions:

COMBINING IDEAS

Sometimes, a great idea can simply be about combining one
or more ideas together. The musical *Hamilton* combines a
historical biography with rap/hip hop and Broadway to produce a fresh concept. Meow Wolf's *House of Eternal Return*
combines the idea of an art installation with an indoor playground. *Star Wars: Rise of the Resistance* in Disneyland and

Disney's Hollywood Studios combines several ride concepts into one "attraction" for a multi-act adventure.

CHANGING PERSPECTIVES

Consider how you can tell your story in a unique way that sets it apart from other experiences. For example, if you were to tell the story of *Alice in Wonderland*, rather than tell it from Alice's point-of-view, what would an experience look like if you were to tell it from the Queen of Hearts' perspective? How does that change the experience?

CHANGING MOOD AND TONE

You can make your experience unique by changing the mood and tone of the story. Imagine taking the story of Little Red Riding Hood and instead of making it into a scary, cautionary tale of sticking to the "safe path," change the mood so it's about the excitement of self-discovery in your path. How does that change your experience? By changing the tone from "be careful where you tread" to "have courage in taking a different path," you have made your experience different and unique.

CHANGING GENRES

In film school, we learned how to take the same scene and write it as a comedy, drama, horror, suspense, mystery or psychological thriller. Perhaps you may consider changing the genre of your experience to find your experience's unique factor. For a dramatic subject matter, can you make it into a suspenseful interactive game?

For example, the *Be Washington* interactive theater experience in George Washington's Mount Vernon invites visitors to step into the boots of George Washington and "come face to face with challenges that he confronted as commander in chief or president" during the Revolutionary War.[57] Dramatic and emotionally engaging, visitors watch one of four key scenarios before taking the opportunity to choose from a panel of advisors to consult with before making their decision in an 18-minute interactive format. The experience takes a historical subject matter in the drama genre and changed it to a suspense genre via an interactive game.

Be Washington at George Washington's Mount Vernon. Photo: Margaret Kerrison

CHANGING THE MEDIUM

Rather than a theatrical show, imagine what your experience will look like as a boat ride. Imagine if *Pirates of the Caribbean* was an immersive, walkthrough experience. Imagine if the *Mad Tea Party* ride was an interactive playground. There are so many ways to express your story by simply altering the genre or medium. Look at things

---

[57] http://play.bewashington.org

differently and you may find that the innovative idea you're looking for was in front of you the whole time.

A STORY ONLY YOU CAN TELL

Ultimately, you want to create an experience that only *you* can do. There can never be another Winchester Mystery House. There is no better place to tell the story of Sarah Winchester and her peculiar remodeling project than at the Winchester House. Underwood Family Farms in Moorpark, California wouldn't be as engaging inside a theme park. Visiting a working farm, riding in tractor-pulled vehicles, and petting live animals are activities your visitors can fully appreciate only at the farm itself. (Please see color photo section.)

Consider how your story is one only *you* can tell. Scratch that. Consider how your story is one only you can tell best.

PUTTING IT INTO WORDS
THE CREATIVE GUIDE

KEY PILLARS

Like building a house, you want to create a strong foundation for your story. These "key pillars" should be captured and written in a deck/document so that it can be easily shared with the team. It's the start of your creative guide and should include your project goals, creative promise, storytelling approach, and other parameters that are specific to your project. These key pillars set your story foundation and serves as the creative intent for your team.

PROJECT GOALS

You want to outline the shared goals of the team in a concise and inspirational manner. I use bullet points to outline what we're trying to achieve creatively as a team. It's a form of "contract" so that every current and future team member will understand exactly what the team is building. There shouldn't be any guesses. The goals should be outlined as clear as day. Many of these goals were probably taking shape during the blue sky/charrette process. Use these goals to hold your team accountable.

CREATIVE PROMISE

What's the promise of your experience? Remember, the promise fulfills your visitor's wish fulfillment. Start with bulletpoints and flesh them out if you'd like, but it should be clear and succinct enough for any team member to understand. In this promise, you can also address the transformation (emotional takeaway) of your visitor. What do you hope they walk away feeling?

STORYTELLING APPROACH

Outline your storytelling approach to create the story framework of your experience. Whether your approach is to encourage all visitors to engage with a childlike curiosity (e.g. Meow Wolf), or to find their inner hero (e.g. *Avengers Campus*), the approach describes your perspective/your unique lens to storytelling. Will you embrace diversity and authenticity? Is it important that your visitor plays an active role in your experience? What are the priorities in your storytelling approach that you want to highlight?

NO RULES

There are no hard and fast rules in developing your key pillars. As a member of the core creative team, you should lead the discussion on what the most important aspects of your project are about. This will be especially helpful for newcomers to the project. After all, the process defines the product. How you communicate your creative intent to the team will influence how your team works towards the final product. If you begin with ambiguity and confusion, then it will show in the product. Begin with clear creative intent and context, and the product will have a higher chance of becoming successful.

DESIGN PHILOSOPHY

Now that you have your key pillars in place, it's time to think about your project's design philosophy. In other words, how do the key pillars manifest into design? How do they translate into architecture, landscape, interior, merchandise, food and beverage, audio, props, characters, and other elements of your experience? None of these elements are randomly selected or placed. The design is purposeful and meaningful and serves a greater purpose to fit into the larger narrative and placemaking.

Joe Rohde put it very eloquently in his presentation titled "Creating Narrative Space" in the ICAM15 conference in Paris (May 2, 2010). Here's an excerpt taken from the transcript of his speech:[58]

> The key rule of visual narrative is to "show" not to "tell." In order for the designer to know that the space will "show" not "tell," decisions about surface appearance must be committed to first, before they are compromised by plan or massing. These cannot be arbitrary or they lose all narrative impact. One of the reasons that so many recent attempts at narrative place-making fail and fall into kitsch, is that the visual narrative system *is in fact* superimposed, and rather late, upon a predetermined functional plan and elevation, rather being than the a priori reason for the plan and elevation. [emphasis Rohde's]

The categories you choose to include in your design philosophy are unique to your project. For a museum exhibit, you may decide to have categories for graphics, copy, and media. Perhaps you'll have categories for the theme, region, art movement, or artist so that you

---

[58] https://www.dix-project.net/item/3490/misc-documents-creating-narrative-space

can set the philosophy for how you choose each item for your exhibit. Ultimately, you want to develop categories that are appropriate for your team. Each category clearly defines the parameters for the designers. For example, if you're building an ancient kingdom, then the choice of the doorknobs in your land would steer towards a more organic material, perhaps wood, rather than a modern satin nickel one.

If you have an entire land or park, you can categorize the Creative Guide into each discipline:

- Architecture
- Landscape Design
- Graphic Design
- Audio Design
- Media Design
- Set/Prop Design
- Music
- Live Entertainment Performers
- Retail
- Food & Beverage
- Employee Role

Start the conversation with the creative director and meet with all the other leads to capture their approach. You'll be surprised how quickly you can determine whether a team is in sync or not. As the story champion, you can communicate the story to each discipline lead in a collaborative way and in return, collect vital information for your Design Philosophy.

READABILITY AND BELIEVABILITY IN WORLDBUILDING

"There are details within details within details to anchor you in the fact that we are talking about the real world, not an illustrated children's book fantasy world."

— *Joe Rohde*[59]

A Design Philosophy translates your story into design that is easy for your audience to understand. At Imagineering, we seek to establish immediate "readability" so that the audience can easily suspend their disbelief. As I mentioned earlier in the book, the suspension of disbelief is a concept that describes how in order to become emotionally involved in a narrative, audiences must react as if the characters are real and the situation/events they find themselves in are happening now, even though they know it is only a fictional story.

By looking at the design, whether virtual or physical, does your experience quickly translate and represent your story and world authentically? Can you suspend your audience's disbelief so that they don't question the imagined world around them?

Building an imagined world involves asking detailed questions and drawing inspiration from the real world. When you travel to a different country, you are immersed in a location with a unique history and background. Consider how you can immerse your guests in your world by filling in the story details to create a fully developed and layered destination.

---

[59] https://www.wikio.org/ne/wiki/joe-rohde-biography-age-earring-animal-kingdom-projects-and-aulani-497884

Consider some of these questions in creating a unique and memorable fictional world:

1) Location

Is your place on Earth? In our solar system? In a fictional universe? Where exactly is it in the universe? Does it have other celestial bodies around it? If so, what? Does the location of the place support a greater significance to the story? If not, can it? What does the planet look like? What's the climate and geography? What are the natural resources?

2) History

What's your world timeline? What are some of the major events that have shaped this place? Was there a singular event that changed the course of the people's everyday lives? How did it affect the people? What were their reactions and responses? Who were the people that lived here 100,000 years ago? 1,000 years ago? 100 years ago? 10 years ago? What was the status quo before the event and how did life change after it?

3) People and Population

What's the makeup of the population? Are there different species, races, and ethnicities? Are there different gender types? Age groups?

4) Political and Social Organization

Is there a government? Rules of politics? What's the social hierarchy? Who's on top and who's at the bottom? Are there sectors/kingdoms/countries/cities/towns? Who's in charge? Were they always in charge? What's their livelihood? Where do they live? How do they live? Alone? In communities? What's their idea of "family" or "community?"

5) Values, Beliefs, Culture and Customs

What are their values and beliefs? Do they have religions or believe in gods? Who are these gods? What's the culture here? What are the customs? Do they have a unique language or manner of speaking? How do they greet each other? Do they have unique gestures? What's their view of the world? What do they eat? How do they eat? What do they do for fun? What are examples of their arts and culture? How do they dress? What are their mannerisms?

6) Rules of the World

Are the rules of the world based on real world laws of physics? Is there magic? If so, what kind of magic and how is it used? Who has magic? Is it desired or feared? Is there a hierarchy for people with magic? Is there a calendar? Is time similar to the real world or is there a different measure of time? Does time work in the same way? If not, how is it different?

It's all in the details. One loose string can unravel the intricate fabric of the world you are trying to create. Examine and scrutinize each story element, ask detailed questions, and poke holes at your world so that you can ensure that every story element belongs and elevates the greater design of your imagined world. By looking at every element through the lens of your story world, you can spot elements that do not belong and work together to redact or revisit them.

Never underestimate the power of your audience's desire to believe. This is why they came to your experience in the first place; to escape and immerse themselves in a believable world that they can enjoy with all of their senses. In designing your experience, you want to make sure that all of the details work in harmony to create this believable illusion; seamless and unbroken.

With *Star Wars: Galaxy's Edge*, we had to establish how quickly visitors could read *Star Wars* in our design. If the answer is "not very easily," then we had to change it. We wanted our visitors to believe that they were in the *Star Wars* universe. We did this by establishing visual cues that read *Star Wars* in every design element in the land, from the trash cans to the restrooms.

One of our favorite rules was the three-second rule, which we learned from Doug Chiang, vice president and executive creative director of Lucasfilm. He, in turn, learned from George Lucas, who used this method to accept and reject designs. If in three seconds, visitors didn't believe that they were looking at something from *Star Wars*, then the design needs to be rejected or changed. That's how quickly it takes for our visitors to read a scene and make sense of it. If you don't establish the readability of your experience, then the believability is compromised. When our visitor walks into the *Millennium Falcon*, that readability must be established in three seconds or less before we risk losing them. Don't give them a reason to stop believing.

ALL IN THE DETAILS — YOUR NOUNS

As human beings, we are pattern recognizers and seekers. When we see something that is "out of pattern," or "out of the norm," we quickly find it. This was a survival mechanism for us. We were able to distinguish that a lion was hiding behind a bush so that we can quickly run away from it. We create patterns in our minds so that we can learn and place meaning to them for future reference.

Everything, from the texture of the pavement to the wall sconces and trash cans, should have a place in the world you're creating. You don't see a modern media display in Frontierland. Disney's Animal Kingdom spares no expense in creating a detailed world that speaks to the "intrinsic value of nature." Disney even ensures that their cast member costumes are themed to the lands.

As we learned in elementary school, a noun is a person, place or thing. Focus on your nouns so that they may support the readability and believability of your world.

PERSON

If you are building an immersive world, every character and employee should be themed to that world. Disney cast members are some of the greatest customer-service employees in the world, creating an environment that is fun, inclusive, safe, courteous, and entertaining. Not only does Disney create unique costumes for cast members in every land, they also ensure that they receive the proper training. They are trained with the authentic story, phrases (or spiels as we call them) so that they know how to communicate to visitors and stay "in-story." All it takes is one bad interaction to "break the story," and we work hard to ensure that our cast members have the tools and creative support to maintain and elevate the story that the team has worked so hard to create.

If you are building a smaller immersive experience, consider how you can train your employees to serve the story. Whether it's training them to learn a few greetings or phrases or even asking them to "play" with visitors for a moment, it makes all the difference in the world. Chances are, your employees are the first interaction your audience makes with your experience. Why not make it fun and engaging?

PLACE

Creating a sense of place or "placemaking," as we call it at Imagineering, is one of the most important things in building an immersive world. Walking into any land, whether it be Fantasyland or Tomorrowland, gives you the feeling of being transported into an entirely different world. With lands like *Cars Land* (please see color photo section), *Pandora – The World of Avatar,* and *Star Wars: Galaxy's Edge,* we have taken immersion and authenticity to a whole new level.

You don't have to build a 14-acre land to create an immersive space. Consider your key pillars and design philosophy. I've seen 10×10 rooms that have more authenticity and immersion than some massive theme parks. Think about the last time you went to a friend's house and admired one of their rooms. What was it about the room that made you feel excited or engaged? Was it their collection of books? Souvenirs from around the world? Or the handmade art that they've created over the years? A space, no matter how small, can tell a story, one detail at a time.

Pandora — The World of Avatar in Disney's Animal Kingdom. Photo: Julia Lopes on Unsplash.

THING

In addition to the people and the place, your project is also defined by the things that your audience will see, touch, and interact with. Consider everything that you place in your project and ensure that it supports your story. Remember that something out of place is going to be perceived as "out of story" by your audience. Why is that important? Because the moment your audience realizes that you don't care about the details, it gives the message that you don't care enough about your work to support the story. The details make all the difference between an average experience and an exceptional one. It was Walt Disney's pursuit of perfection that continues to inspire us every day to achieve that perfection.

PERSON, PLACE, THING WORKING IN HARMONY

I don't know how many times I've heard or read from fans that they appreciated all the little details that were included in *Star Wars: Galaxy's Edge*. There was literally and figuratively no stone left unturned. We worked hard to ensure that everything that you saw, touched, tasted, smelled, and heard was undeniably *Star Wars*.

For example, our audio department did an amazing job creating the soundscape of detailed elements like the TIE fighters flying overhead, coupled with our incredible cast members (or local Batuuans as we call them) reacting to the sounds of the TIEs by ducking their heads and saying that they "fly lower and lower each day." This immersion was created by all of the disciplines working together in harmony, creating an ecosystem that was believable and inspiring. All of that began with our clear and strong vision to create a planet that belonged nowhere else but in the *Star Wars* universe.

SUMMARY – DESIGN PHILOSOPHY

Your project may not be as big as an entire land, but it is worth noting that no matter the scale, the design philosophy is one that should be created to guide your team in creating intent and context for your vision.

For example, if you're developing a themed restaurant, you may choose the categories that are suitable for your design philosophy. This may include the food and drink design and delivery methods, music, textures, graphics, service, and interior design. For each category, you return to your key pillars and establish how each of these elements can be manifested/translated into design. If your

themed restaurant has the goal of transporting custom-
ers to a "dream world," how can you further define your
categories? Is there ethereal music to make your custom-
ers feel like they're floating in air? Is the table not really
a dining table at all, but a projection-mapped surface
that displays different images depending on the customer's chosen dream state? How will they order their food
and drink? How will they experience them? Consider how
your experience is multi-sensory and that every attention
to detail speaks to your story.

Ultimately, you want to clarify the categories of your design
philosophy with the goal of aligning them with your key
pillars. There should be a consistency and synchronicity
in each category that complements one another to make
a greater whole. In other words, each category speaks the
same visual language. With a strong design philosophy
in place, there is less ambiguity in decision-making. As
a designer, if you were to choose between a dark metal
doorknob or a light wooden one to support the "dream
world" concept, you may choose a softer, more organic
material based on your key pillars.

Develop what is appropriate for your project, and determine what is useful for your team members. Meet with
the overall creative director, producer, and all the designers. It's amazing what you can discover through frequent
conversations and by delving deeper into questioning the
creative intent. As the storyteller, your job is to ask the
"whys" of the design. Why do you choose these colors for
the space? Why do you choose this shape for the building?
Who are the visitors as they walk into the experience? Why
did you choose these props and objects? You can bring

up important questions that the team never considered before. In these conversations, you can shape the story of the experience together.

In developing your land design philosophy, rest assured that you can revisit it during your design process. You don't have to establish everything before you start a project. Often times, I returned to the design philosophy to make a few tweaks based on our learnings. We are in such an iterative business that it would be impossible to establish all the principles in the very beginning and not make any changes. All of those learnings, however, should be captured in the design philosophy so that current and future team members have a source to understand your design intent. Setting up context, establishing reasoning for design choices, and giving examples are useful in bringing the team together to fulfill a core mission.

BUT WAIT, THERE'S MORE...

We discussed developing the key pillars and design philosophy, but what else should you include in your Creative Guide? In the television industry, the writers develop what is called a "series bible" or "story bible." This is the blueprint and formal document to the entire TV show to track the characters, arcs, episodes, and seasons. Typically, the writer(s) include the premise of the show, character bios, sample episode summaries, story arcs, and other relevant information to help successfully pitch the show to executives.

In addition to the bible, the writer(s) will also typically include a pilot (first) episode in the pitch packet so that executives can get a solid idea of what the show is about. Once the show is picked up, the bible becomes a living document for writers to track what happens in the show for future writers and team members. It typically runs anywhere from 10-50 pages, but it really depends on the project.

A Creative Guide should serve something similar for your project. It should include a comprehensive walk-through description of the visitor experience. Describe in detail what the visitor sees, hears, touches, smells, tastes, and interacts with as they go through your experience. You may want to break down the experience scene by scene and describe the key details. It's your choice on how deep you want to go in the descriptions. Ultimately, it should describe your experience so well that any person who picks up the guide and reads it should understand what your experience is about.

Here are other chapters/sections that can be included in your Creative Guide:

- Project Team Members/Bios
- Visitor Experience — Scene-by-Scene Breakdown
- Main Characters
- Supporting Characters
- Character Relationships
- Storylines
- Retail Description
- Dining Description
- Entertainment Description
- Seasonal Events
- Private Events

- Ongoing Visitor Participation — How can you keep your visitors involved?
- Multi-platform Storytelling Extensions — Summaries of other formats connected to your experience
- Useful resources
- Fun facts/Easter eggs

Ultimately, you want to create a guide that captures the creative intent in written form. Like a story bible for a television series, it should be informative, comprehensive, but also concise. What are the most important messages you want to convey to the people responsible for upholding, maintaining, and continuing the creative intent? Can you add visuals, graphics, and examples of the important elements?

Your Creative Guide also serves as a useful guide for future creators and team members to create new stories and evolve your story experience into other formats and opportunities. By reading your Guide, they may develop new experiences, off-shoot books, comics, merchandise, food and beverage offerings, marketing initiatives, apps or games. If you've created an experience that is rich and full of possibilities, then the future opportunities are limitless.

THE WRITING DELIVERABLES

What do you mean, you write for immersive entertainment? Do they even need writers for theme parks? What kind of writing do you do? Everyone seems to understand that there are writers for movies, video games, comics, and books. Yet, somehow, most people are surprised by the idea of writers working in immersive entertainment.

Yes, there are writers in immersive entertainment. Story doesn't just happen. The best experiences in the world were written before they were created. There are many creatives and storytellers on any single team, but the writer is the one who captures all of the best ideas into written word. They are the advocate and champion of story. They are responsible for keeping the creative team on track with their story mission and final destination.

Writing happens to be my tool to communicate story. Artists draw, designers design, creative directors direct, producers produce. Writers write. All of us work together as a team to bring our shared story to life in our various disciplines. We all have different deliverables based on our craft and depending on the scope of your project, the deliverables may be unique as well.

As a writer, these are some of the deliverables you may be responsible for during different phases of a project.

Blue sky phase (post-charrette)

After the charrette, writers continue to develop on the big ideas and translate them into the project goal, main theme, key pillars, and design philosophy. Writers are responsible for the research of the stories or topics in development. They may spearhead any initiative to bring in any experts or consultants and gather any necessary information vital to the growth of the project. They write concept statements, summaries, and brief outlines of the visitor experience. They may also be asked to help with writing pitches and talking points for presentations to sell the idea.

Concept/Design phase

During the concept phase, writers define the visitor experience. They begin with a basic concept and work with the core creative team to create a beat sheet, outline, treatment, and eventually a script. In addition to developing the main show, they also help to write other supporting materials for audio, graphics, and media. They work with the team to create nomenclature (names) and stories for the land, attraction, dining, retail, character encounters, and other experiences. If they're building an immersive world, they would create names for characters and their backstories. They would work with any relevant partners to ensure that the stories are authentic, accurate, and engaging.

Production/Implementation phase

Writers continue the process of rewriting any material based on the iterative process of developing the experience. Working with the team, they determine how best to hone in on the story through multiple drafts of the script(s) and other written deliverables such as the Creative Guide. Stories may be tweaked depending on the parameters of the project and may require the writers to capture stories in other formats such as media, images, graphics, charts, and other materials. They revise and finalize all of the scripts for media and graphics copy. The writer ensures that the most current stories are updated and shared with the team.

Installation phase

The writers create additional content for the visitors such as wayfinding, marketing, and communications. They help write the product descriptions sold in the retail locations and write descriptions for food and drink items. During the installation phase, some creative elements may change. It's the writer's responsibility to capture all of the changes and communicate them with the team.

Pre-Opening phase

Writers finish the guide that captures the creative intent of the experience (if it wasn't completed already). They also develop and write training materials for staff members in the form of in-story spiels or informative talking points. They explore unique ways to create a strong hook/pitch to engage their audience.

Opening phase

Writers finally prepare materials for marketing, communications, and talking points for project team members. They may be asked to communicate with the press and appear in media as the story representative of the project.

Post-Opening Sustainment

Writers are responsible for keeping the world/exhibit/ experience alive. They are responsible for keeping the content fresh, relevant, and engaging. They may develop new stories or find new activations for the stories in different formats (e.g. new offerings in dining, merchandise, publishing, virtual/digital, walkaround characters). They may partner with different lines of business to expand the storytelling universe in multiple platforms that help the audience connect and engage in unique ways.

INDUSTRY FORMAT

Many people ask whether there is an industry format in writing for immersive entertainment. The simple answer is no. Besides the industry format for writing screenplays using a professional software such as Final Draft, most of our deliverables are written in a Microsoft Word or Pages document.

We also often use a presentation format such as Keynote or PowerPoint to share our ideas in a group setting. Ultimately, you want to capture the creative intent in a way that will be most useful to your team. It may differ from company to company, so it's best to be open and flexible in your formatting. At the end of the day, you want to present your work in the most professional manner, without any typos, misspellings, or misinformation.

PITCHING, PRESENTING, AND COMMUNICATING

I cannot stress how important it is to practice pitching, presenting, and communicating. As the writer and story lead for your team, you'll be asked to present the story to internal and external partners in a way that's concise, inspiring, and effective. When someone asks you to present the project, your answer should always be a resounding "Yes!"

I remember the exact moment I decided that I needed to come out of my shell and represent my team. It was in the D23 Expo (the biennial exposition event for Disney fans) in 2017. The team leaders asked for volunteers to either present the land model for fans in a scripted format, or they could volunteer to walk the floor and answer any questions. I chose the latter.

During the first day of the Expo, I looked up at one of our junior designers holding court as he presented the land model to a large crowd. It dawned on me that I just missed a huge opportunity. I was given a chance to speak about the project that I was so passionate about and I didn't take it.

I also came to the realization that as an Asian woman, I had to do my part to represent other minorities in creative fields. I thought about the young Asian girl who walked by and didn't see anyone who looked like her presenting to the crowds. I remembered I was that little girl once and reminded myself that it's not easy to become what you don't see in your life.

It's important to do the work well, but also give people the opportunity to meet the face behind the work. From that moment onwards, I said yes to every opportunity to speak about the project. I said yes to small group presentations and to larger auditorium-sized presentations. I knew I made the right choice when two years later, I was on the stage at D23 with other esteemed panelists in the "Inspiring Women Behind *Star Wars: Galaxy's Edge*" panel.

PITCHING — KNOW YOUR AUDIENCE

Over the years, I have learned some great tips for pitching. First and foremost, you have to be positive and passionate about your project. That's a given. The other important tip I've learned is to know your audience. This isn't a new concept, but one that we often overlook when pitching. Who are you pitching to and how can you tailor your pitch so that you speak their language? What do they want? How can you tailor your pitch to present an idea that they'll want? Depending on whether you're pitching to business executives who will potentially fund your project or to a client who is considering your team's creative proposal, remember to make them feel that they're going to be part of a winning team. Everyone wants to feel like a winner. You want them walking away without a doubt in their mind that they want to be a part of this team.

PRESENTING — KNOW YOURSELF

I got a great tip from Chris Beatty, an Executive Creative Director at Walt Disney Imagineering, who I believe is one of the best presenters I've ever seen. Not only is his passion and enthusiasm contagious from the moment he starts speaking, he also presents what he knows.

I asked him about his secret to presenting. He pointed to a concept art on the wall for what later became Black Spire Station in *Star Wars: Galaxy's Edge*. He answered that you should pitch from your expertise. He explained that as a designer, he would present the concept art by talking about how the light hits the façade and creates a feeling of grandeur and how he chooses the colors to create a sense of warmth. As a writer, however, I should present it through story. How a visitor walks into this space invited by the mystery of the landspeeders and wanting to see what they can find in the nooks and crannies of the space. How their imagination will take flight just by looking at the objects and wondering who runs the place and why they are here. When presenting, lean in on your expertise and present what you know.

Landspeeders at *Star Wars: Galaxy's Edge* in Disneyland. Photo: Rod Long on Unsplash.

COMMUNICATING – KNOW YOUR TEAM

I've learned over the years that effectively communicating with your team means respecting and acknowledging their individual expertise in the project, and finding ways to make the story work from a place of curiosity and learning. In my experience, this transparency is vital to communicating and, ultimately, collaborating with your team. Put aside your ego to listen and learn. Communicating isn't only about speaking and presenting well, it's about listening to your team members so that you can learn and better inform your creative decisions.

Over the years, I've worked with people of varying disciplines, from graphic designers to audio engineers, and I've learned so much from them. In communicating with them, I approach my conversations from a place of curiosity. I welcome educating myself about their discipline and how best to represent the story through their medium. They are the experts in the fields, after all. I always strive to better understand the medium so that I may use it to the story's advantage. We're all reaching for the same goal, which is to create the best possible outcome for the project. So why not use their strengths and expertise to fulfill a shared goal? It's a win-win situation.

PASSING THE TORCH

Y ou've done your duty as the story lead and writer for the concept, design, and installation phases, but your work also includes training and educating the team that will uphold the creative integrity of your experience. You will move on to other projects, but you want to ensure that all of the hard work you and the team have put into the experience is sustained successfully and, perhaps, has the flexibility to be modified or upgraded should the time arise.

At Disney, we have a useful tool called the Show Information Guide. This is the creative guide for the experience, whether it be for a restaurant, shop, attraction, or land, where the writer captures all of the creative and story intent into one single document for all cast members to refer to for the lifespan of that experience.

A version of this Guide can be created for all kinds of locations, from museums to national parks. It's a tool for all staff members to understand how to communicate the origin, history, story, and experience to all visitors. The last thing you want is for the staff members to relay the wrong story or information to future visitors. That is why they are so integral in "passing the torch" as story torchbearers of the experience.

The Guide also serves as a window into the creative mind-set of the original designers and storytellers. What was their creative intent? Why did they make certain creative decisions? Why did they choose this destination? Why did they choose to tell this story? Who are the characters visitors will meet and why? What will visitors do and experience? What is my place in the story? What is the role of the visitors?

There are many chapters and categories you can include in your Guide, depending on the type of experience. The *Star Wars: Galaxy's Edge* Creative Guide ran over 220 pages, which included images and other helpful visual assets. This Guide was integral in communicating with our Cast Members as well as other partners who were interested in extending the stories of our land to games, publishing, merchandise, dining, live entertainment, and other initiatives.

There are many different supporting materials you can incorporate in your Guide, including, but not limited to, cast member role, fun facts, interesting stats and figures, quotes from the original design team, infographics and other helpful visuals and diagrams, background information, and even a glossary of important terms.

The intent is not to make the Guide so cumbersome and tediously long that no one will read it. The purpose is to create a concise, informative, and engaging Guide that will encourage your staff to read and appreciate the experience's creative intent. If you win over your staff, then you win over your visitors. Passion and enthusiasm are contagious. Encourage your staff to pass it on!

CAST MEMBER SPIEL

Another terrific tool we use at Imagineering are cast member spiels. Spiels are not scripts (because our cast members aren't trained professional actors), but they offer guidelines and parameters for our cast members to play in our worlds and engage with our guests. They offer important information and suggested responses for our cast members, so that they have all the tools they need to support the believability and authenticity of the world.

Led by our talented creative director Cory Rouse and our all-star producer Rachel Sherbill, the team developed a detailed and comprehensive cast member engagement program in our Disney Parks to ensure that our cast members could fully engage in the stories that we created.

Inspired by Lucasfilm's Vice President and Creative Director, Doug Chiang, we used an 80/20 rule when training our cast members. In the design of the film *Rogue One*, Doug wanted to make 80% of their designs feel like George Lucas' classic designs and "the other 20% would come from blending the prequel designs with a more handcrafted look."[60]

Our rule of thumb was that our cast members would draw 80% of their dialogue from their real lives and 20% would be drawn from the *Star Wars* universe. This way, they didn't have to fully improvise their interactions with guests. We wanted to ensure that their interactions felt as authentic as possible, which meant that they could draw inspiration from their own lives. Talking about your own life is a lot easier than making one up in a fictional world.

---

[60] https://www.starwars.com/news/swco-2017-10-things-we-learned-from-doug-chiangs-rogue-one-panel

Market at *Star Wars Galaxy's Edge* in Disneyland. Photo: Margaret Kerrison

For example, if a cast member lived with a family of four and owned dogs in real life, they would still live with a family of four and own dogs. However, they would be living on the planet Batuu and would simply refer to their dogs as "hounds."

If they lived in the suburbs in real life, we had an equivalent Batuuan community that shared similar characteristics with their real home (e.g. living in a big house versus an apartment). If they had certain hobbies and skills like fishing for bass, tinkering with cars in the garage, and programming code, we had *Star Wars* equivalents of those hobbies and skills, like fishing for Burra fish, tinkering with a landspeeder, and programming droids.

At the start of every training, each cast member developed their own profile based on their family, background, experiences, livelihood, hobbies, and personality. In training cast members to engage as local Batuuans, our goal was to make them feel comfortable enough to talk about their own lives within the context of Batuu. They didn't need to be a *Star Wars* expert to engage in this world. They ultimately needed to learn new nouns (e.g. hounds, landspeeders, droids), but the verbs remained the same (e.g. fishing, tinkering, programming).

YOU AS A WRITER

In most other writing professions, you are told to find your unique voice and "write what you know." This may be true if you are writing for yourself. If you're working on a novel, screenplay, a collection of short stories, or poems that represent a unique story only you can tell, then the answer is yes, find your voice and write what you know.

In immersive storytelling, however, you are assigned a subject that you must authentically represent in an emotionally engaging way. You have to be open and adaptable as a storyteller. There are some subjects that may be of more interest to you, but at the end of the day, you're a professional writer who will bring passion into every topic that you're presented with. Take every project as a welcome challenge to tell stories that you've never told before.

I've written stories for experiences about beer, an old state capitol, wildlife, rocket science, cosmetics, K-pop, the history of telecommunications, Bollywood, the weather, superheroes, and the Jedi, just to name a few. As the storyteller, it is your responsibility to find the passion and your connection to the subject. Answer the question of "why should I care?" and you can help others find the compelling and deeper meaning of any topic.

KNOW THYSELF

While you should aspire to have the ability to tell any kind of story on any subject in any format, it's also important to know your strengths and interests. When you're meeting with other professionals in the industry, have a good idea of what stories speak to you and understand why.

Learn to talk about some of your favorite stories, attractions, and experiences. Most importantly, learn to talk about what motivates you. Develop a personal motto.

Here's my motto: "Awaken Minds through the Power of Storytelling."

No matter what project I'm on, this is my goal. To awaken people's minds through the power of storytelling. I want to send chills down their spines, bring tears of joy to their eyes, shake them awake, and transform them. That's the kind of storytelling I'm interested in.

As an "experiences enthusiast," it's always a good idea to try out different kinds of experiences, so that you know what kind of experiences appeal to you. It's also important to be familiar with what's out there, so you can have a better understanding of the comparables and competition. Screenwriters watch other TV shows and films. Novelists read other novels. Experience designers partake in other experiences. Be a curious learner of the format and absorb as much as you can.

Know yourself as a writer by asking these questions:

1) What's your personal motto? What drives you?

2) What are five of your favorite stories/experiences/ attractions of all time?

3) Why do these stories and experiences appeal to you?

4) In your top five, are there any recurring stories, genres, or themes?

5) What's the most recent experience you attended? What did you think of it? Why did you feel that way?

6) What's a story you want to share with the world?

If you can easily answer these questions, then you're well on your way to knowing who you are as a storyteller. If you know who you are as a storyteller, then you have the power to transform your audience.

As I mentioned in an earlier chapter,

**Find a little bit of yourself in the story,
and your audience will find a little bit of the story in
themselves.**

WRITING AS A PROFESSION

As a writer working in a multi-disciplinary team, you want to bring a positive, can-do attitude to the project. You are the "heart" of the team; the one who understands the greater meaning of the experience. As the storyteller, you represent the story of the experience like no one else can. You must learn to communicate the story in a clear, compelling, and emotionally engaging way. Your role is to provide thematic clarity to a team. If the team is struggling to understand the big idea, then it's your responsibility to work with the creative director to guide the team to its creative goal.

Every team member is pressed for time and has their own priorities and responsibilities. We want to help each other in times of need so that we can work together towards a shared goal. This doesn't mean that you give up your personal life and boundaries. It means that you should offer to help a team member and work hard together, especially in the most stressful and challenging phases of the project. The best projects I've worked on were the ones in which the project leaders and team members had my back, and vice versa. The job is hard enough as it is. It's better to do it with the support of your team.

At the end of the day, our individual names aren't going to be showcased or highlighted on the big screen, a billboard, or on a book cover. In this industry, it's all about the team. You are part of a creative engine that moves the project forward in every step of the process. One broken part in the engine and the whole thing slows down or falls apart. Be the person that others can depend on, but ask for help when you need it. Be sure to ask for context and clarification on the priority of a task. If someone is asking for something that you don't have the skill or knowledge for, then ask questions or request help or resources.

Your reputation in one job will last longer than you can ever imagine. In the minds of your project team members, how you perform in one job will determine whether or not they will call you back for the next job. You're building your reputation as a storyteller and writer. One brick at a time, you're establishing the kind of a professional that you are. Based on your performance in the current project, other professionals will decide whether you're someone they want to build their house with or without.

This is a small world and an even smaller industry. You want to strive to be the person everyone thinks about when they're putting together a creative team. You want to be a team player who is kind, responsible, trustworthy, hard-working, and flexible. You want to be many other things, but you should strive to be these things first and foremost. No one wants to work with a difficult personality, no matter how awesome and talented you are in your craft. There is no time and energy for big egos, no matter how many years you've worked in the industry. The team shouldn't have to focus their time and energy on challenging personalities when the work is challenging enough.

HOW DO YOU BREAK INTO THIS INDUSTRY?

There is no one sure way for you to break into this industry. I know that's not what you want to hear, but it's the truth. Every single writer I've met in my career got their first breaks in different ways. However, here are a few suggestions to help you in your journey.

1) Write in your free time.

Writers write. There's no way around it. Even if you don't have a job, you should spend most of your time writing. Write about anything. Write about nothing. Write a short story, poem, screenplay, the next great American novel. Writing is a craft and takes hours and hours of practice. Like an athlete or musician, you must take time in your craft and learn to be disciplined.

You must also learn to be a versatile and adaptable writer. In addition to screenwriting, learn to write environmental descriptions, short form content, interactive media, audio scripts, and product descriptions. All of these forms of writing will come in handy in your role.

One of the characteristics that a company seeks in a writer is your ability to adapt and be flexible in your storytelling. You may rewrite a ten-minute show into a graphics copy on a plaque. You may write a show that has to change in tone, character voice, and/or location. You may be required to write descriptions for a product or a marketing brochure. You may even write lyrics to a song.

Take the time to develop some killer writing samples — everything from advertising writing to environmental descriptions to family entertainment/comedy scripts. Other great writing examples include scripts and other written materials for games, comic books, websites, and other formats that show your range and diversity as a writer. Also, be aware of the hiring company's IP and genres. You wouldn't want to send an adult comedy script or a horror writing sample to a family entertainment company. Only send your *best* work. You get one chance to make a first impression.

2) Start with freelance work.

When I was still a grad student at USC, I took on freelance writing jobs in animation companies outside of the United States. Because I wasn't a Writer's Guild Association member, this was the only way for me to get a paid writing job. Freelance jobs are a great way to break into paid writing gigs. The company doesn't have to employ you full-time and they can "try you out" before committing. The same goes for you. You can "try out" a company before committing to them.

As a freelancer/consultant, you can take on multiple jobs in various industries so you can get a better idea of what kind of work or industry suits your skills and interests. I freelanced with animation, production, education, and design companies. It was a great way for me to determine what I was (and wasn't) interested in. I quickly figured out that I wasn't interested in technical writing (which is a very lucrative job and is in very high demand these days!). I also figured out that I was very interested in writing for children and family entertainment. I don't think I ever grew out of my childlike mentality and perspective, which comes in very handy when you're working on experiences targeted for the whole family.

If you're just starting out in this industry, it's also a great way to gain some experience and meet new people. You'll also have a writing goal. Plus, if you're lucky enough to have your work produced or published, then it becomes a solid sample of work for your portfolio. A portfolio, no matter how small, is better than not having any work to showcase your talents.

3) Network and build connections.

This is a tough one because as an introvert, I am one of those people who hates going to networking events and mixers. Networking in this industry, however, is so important. As I mentioned before, this is a small world and an even smaller industry. Most of the work I gained as a writer was through personal connections and "word of mouth." Most of the writing jobs aren't advertised. All the more reason for you to meet as many people as you can in this industry and learn as much as you can.

If you're going to a networking or other industry event like IAAPA (The International Association of Amusement Parks and Attractions Expo), go with a friend. Meet someone over e-mail or a phone chat and if you've made a connection, ask if you can meet them at an industry event and have them introduce you and your friend to other professionals.

What's important to keep in mind, however, is that you don't go to these meetings asking for a job. What you should do, however, is request an informational meeting or "meet and greet." Let people know that you're very interested in what they do in the industry and would like to set up a half hour coffee chat to talk about their experiences. Most people would be happy to set up a phone or in-person chat, as their busy schedules allow. What works best is if you have a referral. "So-and-so told me I should get in touch with you to talk about what you do."

I often have "meet-and-greets" with aspiring Imagineers and writers, but I rarely hire someone I've never personally worked with before or who wasn't highly recommended to me from someone I trust. That is why you should go into these meetings with a curious mindset of asking thoughtful questions rather than directly asking for a job. Don't just meet people to check it off the list of "things to do," but rather, think about asking them questions that will help you determine if this is the right career choice for you.

Often times, your impression of the work is very different from the reality. Meeting with different professionals from the industry will give you real insight into the day-to-day workings of this very rewarding, but highly demanding career.

Be ready to talk about your favorite experiences and why they are your favorites. If anything, show your passion for the industry. You're meeting with like-minded people who went into this industry for a reason. Share your passions and maybe you'll make a meaningful connection with the right person. Be yourself. It's not an interview, but you should come in as someone the person potentially sees as a peer and colleague one day.

4) Embrace your passion. Be part of the community. There are so many immersive storytelling enthusiasts who are making an impressive effort in sharing their passion by setting up speaker panels, YouTube channels, publishing reviews and articles, setting up podcasts, and building their social media presence. If you're tech and social media savvy, this is a really great way to get noticed by people in the industry. Develop enough of a following and who knows, maybe we'll be the ones knocking on *your* door to invite you to special openings and events in exchange for your thoughtful and honest reviews.

As an influencer, you can share your passions, interview people you admire, and experience all the newest attractions for your audience. What better way to get into the industry than as a fan? If you're a student, start an organization in your school or university. If you have skills directing and editing, start your own YouTube channel or web series. The possibilities are endless.

5) Keep learning.
As an aspiring storyteller in this industry, commit your time to becoming a student of the craft and the industry. Experience everything and be ready to talk about it. Be a curious learner and try to understand what makes a good story. There's always something to learn, even in the "bad" experiences. You may find yourself learning more from

the bad experiences than the good ones. Why didn't it work? What would you do to improve it?

Furthermore, inspiration comes from everywhere. Read books, watch movies, support your local performing arts theaters, explore your city parks. A curious mind will lead you down many interesting paths.

I've been in this profession for 14 years and I'm still learning. Every time I go to a new experience, there's always a takeaway. I see every experience as a learning opportunity in which to think differently. Never stop learning.

WHY WE DO WHAT WE DO

I woke up this morning and reached over for my book. I turned on some relaxing music and laid in bed, engrossed in words. Then I started thinking about why I loved reading, and I realized it was one of the few times in the day that I'm actually present. Reading, writing, practicing yoga, traveling, hiking, going to museums and experiences, watching movies, playing games, and enjoying good food and wine. All of these activities keep me in the present moment. I'm fully focused on one thing and not thinking about anything else.

We're constantly distracted. We have a need to always produce or consume. Ask yourself, when was the last time you did *a single* thing at a time? When was the last time you ate without watching something on TV or on your computer? When was the last time you just stood in a line without having to reach for your phone? We can't even get into an elevator and go up two floors without reaching for our phones. I'm guilty of this too. When I drive for more than twenty minutes, I have to turn on an audiobook or a podcast. Why are we in such a panicked hurry to always be doing something?

We have this constant need of "doing." We're not giving ourselves enough headspace. As humans, we need to have idle time and occasionally be bored and unproductive. It's good for us! Studies have shown that being bored is actually a good thing. It allows us to be creative. Not only that, but it lets us be alone with our thoughts so we can hear what we have to tell ourselves. Maybe our body is trying to tell us something. Maybe your mind has been shouting at you for something but you were too busy to pay attention. Being unproductive is a great way to hit the reset button at the end of the day.

With so many brands and companies competing for our time and attention, immersive storytelling is continually changing and expanding. It's important to understand that when people go to your experience, they are choosing to pay attention and to be present. They have committed their time, money, and attention to your experience. They want to share a special experience with their family and/ or friends, and do something together and create memories that last a lifetime. They want to make connections with one another that they can't get anywhere else.

That's a huge honor and privilege for anyone working in immersive storytelling. To hear children's laughter, people's screams from a thrilling ride, and witness the tears of joy and wonder in people's eyes — that's why we do what we do. We, as storytellers, are here to bring joy and magic into people's lives. No matter what they're going through in their own lives, when they go to their favorite themed land or attraction or experience, they come to forget, escape, have fun, be together, be happy, and be present.

Right before we opened *Star Wars: Galaxy's Edge* to the public, I remember one evening I took a moment to sit down and look around the land. I was overcome with emotion. I had been running around and trying to get everything done on time, that I didn't stop to appreciate all the hard work we had put into the land. I was proud, happy, relieved, and sad all at once. We had built something great and we were very much looking forward to sharing it with the world, but it was over. It was a bittersweet moment. I had never been prouder of a project before. I hope that in your career, you'll have many moments like these. As stressful and challenging as this industry can be, the reward of seeing how people react to your experience, is priceless.

THE FUTURE OF STORYTELLING IN IMMERSIVE EXPERIENCES

During the COVID-19 pandemic, people were staying at home to work, play, learn, and discover the world around them via remote learning, games, online channels, and streaming platforms. There was also an increasing trend for people to stay closer and more local in their travels.

People explored their local playgrounds, parks, local businesses, and neighborhoods more than ever before, making sure that their family's health and safety came first. There was a boom in domestic travel as people were desperate to get out of the house by safely traveling in their cars. National parks, beaches, hiking trails, bike trails, campsites, and other outdoor recreational sites became popular destinations. Families with children also became more cautious about how they spent their time and money, instigated by a climate in which traveling to theme parks, planning for big vacations, eating out, and in-store shopping became physically and financially challenging, if not impossible.

Coming out of isolation, we have witnessed a great desire for people to socialize and connect on a physical and meaningful level again. In a time when parents were overly dependent on screens to entertain their children at home, there is a strong and renewed desire to reintroduce their kids to experiences that involve playful discovery, multisensory exploration, social interactions, and physical movement. There is also a desire for parents to play with their children again in fun, short-term activities and experiences that don't take up a significant portion of their day. With schedules that are no doubt quickly filling up again with school events, social commitments, and afterschool activities, families desire more opportunities to spend time with their children in limited chunks of time (two to three hours) before moving on to the next event of their day.

We'll probably see continued temperature screenings, face masks, and a greater desire for people to experience things in the comfort of their homes. So many things have become easier to accomplish from home than they were before the pandemic. Online shopping and delivery, remote learning, working from home, consuming entertainment, even socializing via Zoom, have become the norm. We've created habits that have become our daily routines, and many of us will choose to keep some of these habits. I personally want to keep the habit of going for my daily walks and reading voraciously.

Meow Wolf's *Omega Mart* in Las Vegas responded to the pandemic by installing elbow scanners rather than palm readers, among other safety and health precautions. What changes and additions will you make in your experience?

BLURRING THE LINES

"We're pushing the limits of imagination and innovation....
We'll actually blur the lines for our visitors between
fantasy and reality...."

— *Bob Iger*[61]

We're already witnessing humanity's desire to expand upon the limitless potential of storytelling. As audiences become more sophisticated and inundated with choices, they are seeking new ways to partake, escape, and immerse themselves in unique experiences.

We are no longer only entertained by reading books, watching plays/films/TV shows, and attending museums and other events. We are seeking to blur the lines between different media to experience a world or a story as an active participant and perhaps to influence it. Like playing a video game, we desire to have control over our actions and observe the consequences of our actions in a safe environment. Even if our desired level of engagement is to merely explore or observe, we want to be in the "place where it happens" and immerse ourselves fully in our fantasies with fewer barriers. We can be whoever we want to be in a different world. It's the ultimate fantasy.

This fantasy or wish fulfillment stems from our great need to create, share, influence, and connect with others. Many of us already use YouTube, Facebook, Snapchat, TikTok, Instagram, LinkedIn, and other forms of social media as platforms to create our own expressions via messages, photos, videos, and sharing of content. When we spend

---

[61] https://www.wral.com/galaxys-edge-is-a-star-wars-fantasy-and-what-disney-does-best/18419230/

hours scrolling through our feed, following friends and complete strangers, creating our own personas, posting our observations of the world to the world, we are creating a world we want to live in. We have a deep desire to extend our real lives into the digital realm, so that it could extend the identity of the person we think we are or hope to be some day. It's a fun and easy experience that offers our wish to create, influence, connect with others, and ultimately, escape to a different world. We never grew up from our childhood desire to play pretend and try out different costumes to experience what it's like to be someone else.

We can witness this growing idea of a "metaverse" in which we blur the lines between the real and virtual, where there's a digital/AR layer to the real world, or live in an alternate digital reality. A popular example is *Fortnite*, the massively popular multi-player Battle Royale game created by Epic Games and played by some 250 million people around the world. *Fortnite* players attended a virtual concert in 2019 where 100 people at a time could interact with one another. It may not seem like much, but this is where storytelling or "story living" is happening.

We're seeing a dramatic shift in consumer patterns. It's no longer appealing for younger generations to get into a car and drive to a place to experience a story (or watch a concert, in this case). Gone are the days of picking up your friends in their houses, driving in rush hour traffic, finding parking, waiting in line to get into the concert venue, waiting for the main act, paying astronomical prices for drinks and food, and finding a good place to stand or sit without being disturbed by other concertgoers. This

Fortnite concert takes away all the pinch points, so that you can maximize your enjoyment and do exactly what the experience promises — to enjoy an amazing concert with your friends. Since then, Epic Games has offered a concert series with different performing artists, most recently, a collaboration with Ariana Grande.[62]

Blurring the lines between the physical and virtual is growing exponentially in physical locations too. We witnessed the popularity of the immersive virtual reality experience the VOID which showed up in malls all over the world.

I tried three of their experiences (*Ghostbusters: Dimensions, Star Wars: Secrets of the Empire,* and *Ralph Breaks the Internet*). For someone with a small frame and who suffers from motion sickness and claustrophobia, this would probably be the last thing that I'd try out, but I was so intrigued by the promise of the experience. I got over the fact that I had to wear a very heavy headset and vest system and carry a blaster. The best part was working with my friends as a team. No matter which IP we were playing, we felt like we were some elite strike force team on a mission, protecting each other's backs, laughing, and communicating with each other to perform our tasks successfully. At the end of the experience, we'd pose and take a photo together to remember our perilous adventure together.

Over the years, the international art collective, teamLab, has successfully created multiple immersive art installations that break the boundaries between the self and the environment. On their website, they describe their collective as "an interdisciplinary group of various specialists

---

[62] https://www.epicgames.com/fortnite/en-US/news/fortnite-presents-the-rift-tour-featuring-ariana-grande

installations that break the boundaries between the self and the environment. On their website, they describe their collective as "an interdisciplinary group of various specialists such as artists, programmers, engineers, CG animators, mathematicians and architects whose collaborative practice seeks to navigate the confluence of art, science, technology, and the natural world."[63] Unlike numerous experiences around the world that create "immersive art" for the sake of selfie moments, teamLab is doing something different — creating art to "understand the world around them." Their design is driven by art, story, and most importantly, meaning and purpose.

As teamLab founder, Toshiyuki Inoko, said in a New York Times interview[64],

> By connecting digital technology and art, I think it's possible to make other people's existence more positive. Technology is humanitarian. The concept of the digital is to expand the expression of humanity. If that means believing in changing the value system, then maybe it is a form of faith.

We're also seeing a huge trend in augmented reality (AR) games at home. With games like Nintendo Switch's *Mario Kart Live: Home Circuit*[65], players race laps with a camera-mounted, remote-controlled toy car through actual cardboard gates and turn their floor space into Mario Kart race tracks using augmented reality. There is already an increasing desire to blur the lines of the real with the unreal. Soon, we'll be questioning what is "real" anymore. Who says that if you can't touch it, it's not real?

---

[63] https://www.teamlab.art/about/
[64] https://www.nytimes.com/2016/02/04/t-magazine/art/teamlab-living-digital-space-future-parks-pace-gallery-california.html
[65] https://www.nintendo.com/products/detail/mario-kart-live-home-circuit-mario-set/

In addition to playing AR games at home, I can imagine a future in which we return to physical locations and use AR to view pop-up facts of the history, art, architecture, and stories in a historical site or museum. Or perhaps we can hold up our smart phones to see AR elements in the places that we thought we knew. I can imagine going to the Pennsylvania State House (now called Independence Hall), holding up my phone, and witnessing in real time, the signing of the Declaration of Independence. Imagine visiting Emperor Qinshihuang's Mausoleum Site Museum in Xi'an China and witnessing the Terracotta Army come to life in AR.

We want to experience a story wherever, whenever, and however we want. We want options and different ways to engage with our favorite worlds, characters, and stories in new and convenient ways. This "mixed reality," or "meta-verse" as some people call it, is a convergence of the real and virtual worlds. It is becoming easier for us to partake in experiences that were once unattainable, cumbersome, or expensive. The "friction" of the decision-making process has been drastically reduced, which brings us to the next point in the future of immersive experiences.

REDUCING "FRICTION"

Consider the amount of time, energy, and financial investment in planning a week-long trip to Orlando for a family. The time spent planning and scheduling flights, hotels, meals, park tickets, and other events is an epic event in itself! How can you help families with their planning and reduce "friction" in their decision-making? How can you help them experience stories in a convenient, yet unique way?

Companies like Netflix, Amazon, Facebook, Apple, and Google have succeeded in decreasing friction in our lives by "nudging" us towards a certain direction, and sometimes even making the decisions for us. Netflix has a 10-second countdown and autoplay of the next episode. Amazon offers every kind of product in a "Buy Now" click for one-day delivery. Facebook recommends ads based on your search history. Apple's well-designed products make it intuitive and fun to use. Google develops curated search results for every individual user. It can even recommend things we might like by analyzing our search results.

Issues of ethics and privacy aside, it's undeniable that these companies have forever changed our perspective of the customer experience. We are used to decision-making being instant and easy. How can you take a page from these successful companies and make experiences that are easy and irresistible? How can you, as a storyteller, create experiences that offer something that no one else can? How can you build a world that keeps your audience coming back for more?

The Guggenheim in Bilbao, Spain, the Natural History Museum in London, and even the Vatican Museums in Rome are some of the museums that have embraced new technology to offer 360-degree views and virtual tours of their spaces, all from the comfort of your home.

Airbnb's Online Experiences[66] includes everything from pasta making classes with an Italian grandma to meditat-

---

[66] https://www.airbnb.com/s/experiences/online

ing with a monk in Japan. We can experience anything from the comfort of our own homes with anyone from anywhere in the world. Where you are located doesn't matter anymore. The world has become even smaller.

Now more than ever, it's so much easier to visit the places that we never thought we'd visit. We can go around the world and visit well-renowned sites in the comfort of our homes. These advances in technology have also spurred new platforms in which we can experience stories in new and unique ways. They have become open, flexible, and evolving jumping-off points for more stories.

JUMPING-OFF POINT FOR MORE STORIES

In *Star Wars: Tales from the Galaxy's Edge — Parts I and II*[67] (the action-adventure VR experience created by ILMxLAB in collaboration with Oculus Quest), players can visit all the locations in *Star Wars: Galaxy's Edge* and explore other areas not visible in the themed land. Players discover new characters, stories, and locations on the planet of Batuu and embark on new missions and adventures. The team expanded upon the built land to create areas and experiences unachievable in the physical form. They sought to build a VR land that was a storytelling platform and jumping-off point for future stories.

The story possibilities for *Star Wars: Galaxy's Edge* are endless and will continue long after the original creators of this land have moved on to other endeavors. Like George Lucas, who handed others the gift of his original films, future creators are able to expand upon his and other

---

[67] https://www.ilmxlab.com/tales/

creators' *Star Wars* stories in new and engaging ways. Consider how *The Mandalorian* has taken the world by a storm. The original creator, George Lucas, created a world so rich and compelling, that it inspired other creators like Jon Favreau and Dave Filoni to create other unforgettable characters and stories.

Gone are the days of telling a story that is authored by one creator and developed for only one medium. As a creator, it's important to keep your mind open to future stories and platforms that other creators can further expand upon your world. These platforms provide new opportunities of engagement for your audiences. Furthermore, these new stories keep your experience fresh and relevant for future generations.

We have seen how popular books, films, and TV shows get adapted into immersive experiences (franchises like *Star Wars, Jurassic Park, Harry Potter, Transformers, The Simpsons*). The source material doesn't only come from these media anymore, but also from a variety of great storytelling content such as video games. There's *TRON Lightcycle Power Run* at Shanghai Disneyland[68] and an entire land in the form of *Super Nintendo World* at Universal Studios Japan[69]. Creativity inspires more creativity. Richly imagined worlds are the perfect jumping-off point for more stories.

---

[68] https://www.shanghaidisneyresort.com/en/attractions/tron-lightcycle-power-run/
[69] https://www.usj.co.jp/web/en/us/areas/super-nintendo-world

Super Nintendo World at Universal Studios Japan. Photo: Roméo A. on Unsplash.

Your audience (especially the younger ones) may not necessarily distinguish one platform from the other. In their minds, it's one story experienced in different ways. Their action may vary (watching vs playing vs riding, and so on), but the fantasy world remains the same. How can you engage with your younger audience in ways that are seamless and desirable?

It will probably take another decade or so before we enter the realm of Netflix's *Black Mirror* in which the virtual and physical worlds are truly indistinguishable, but the possibility of it happening sooner rather than later is becoming inevitable. Are you ready for it?

DESIRING MEANINGFUL CONNECTION

As humans, we crave meaningful connection. We crave it in every single interaction that we make with others and seek it in the world around us. Every time we interact with someone, we have a desire to be seen and to be heard. Many of us find it in our neighborhoods, workplaces, schools, churches, volunteer groups, and other organizations. Many of us continue seeking that place where we can be ourselves and connect with like-minded people who share a common interest, purpose, or passion. They seek this meaningful connection to better understand themselves, others, and their place in the world.

When your audience pays for an experience, they hope for a meaningful connection and emotional bond with the world experience itself and with the people that they're with and around. There's no surprise about it. Audiences crave experiences to share these moments and create memories with others. We, as creators, should not lose sight of the fact that we tell stories because we want to connect with our audiences and have them connect with one another. This need for meaningful connection drives our audience to seek more experiences in places where they feel like they belong.

Our Disney parks offers a safe, fun, and idyllic world in which cast members, actors, performers, and visitors can connect in fun and meaningful ways. From every cast member to every actor and performer that delight our visitors, we ensure that each interaction with a child or adult is special. We ensure that all of our visitors are "seen" and "heard." It doesn't matter whether you're visiting from another country or driving across the freeway to get to our parks. You are guaranteed a meaningful connection the moment that you arrive. You are exuberantly welcomed, taken care of, and sent off with a smile. Every interaction with a Disney cast member is unforgettable and meaningful, or at least we strive for it to be! Is this the reason why our guests keep returning to our Parks? Disney Parks have become a "main street," a hometown for all kinds of people, regardless of where they're from. It's an inviting and nostalgic place where they feel at home, safe, and connected to a community of people with shared values and interests.

The French composer Claude Debussy once said, "Music is the space between the notes."[70] I strongly believe that our cast members represent this space. As visitors go from one attraction to another throughout their day, they create these small yet magical moments of connection with our cast members. It's a "check in" of sorts." "Are you having a magical day?" "Is there anything I can do for you?" These are all ways in which we ensure that our audience experience is nothing less than wonderful.

The future of experiences will embrace this meaningful connection. It already has, and it will only continue to grow. We're trying to find meaning in everything that we do — our jobs, our personal lives, our friends and families, our social media, our hobbies and interests. We crave this connection with others in both the physical and virtual spaces. The challenge is, how to make each and every one of these connections a meaningful one. You can help them.

---

[70] https://en.wikiquote.org/wiki/Claude_Debussy

SHARING SMALLER, MORE SEAMLESS EXPERIENCES

I imagine there will be a greater audience desire to partake in more intimate, customized, and collaborative experiences. These experiences create a story world that is shared by a small group of people in an environment that is controlled and curated. Lines of businesses (dining, retail, hospitality, leisure & entertainment) will be blended into one seamless, shared experience. I think of Savi's Workshop — Handbuilt Lightsabers in *Star Wars: Galaxy's Edge* and Ollivanders Wand Shop in *The Wizarding World of Harry Potter* where retail and entertainment are blended into a unique and memorable experience.

We'll have the opportunity to explore this next-gen version of a more intimate, seamless, and interconnected experience in *Star Wars: Galactic Starcruiser* in Orlando, Florida. The experience blends various lines of businesses to create an integrated experience for all of its visitors or "passengers" as we call them. Whether you decide to play holo-sabacc in the lounge or partake in activities on the Bridge, each experience is designed for smaller groups. What you decide to do will also influence the rest of your adventure. It will be an experimental, one-of-a-kind experience where audiences can connect with other "passengers," the crew members (our staff), and the characters (live performers) in a wider, interconnected storyline.

When you think of attending a party of thousands vs an intimate dinner party, which sounds like a more inviting experience to you? In a world where we're seeking more connection than ever, I wonder if themed experiences will become smaller in scale, so that the audience can feel "special" and "connected."

In a previous chapter, I mentioned going to a little gem of an experience called *The Willows*, an immersive theater experience that included entertainment, drinks, and small bites for up to eighteen visitors. The experience clearly didn't have a single linear narrative, but I walked away from it feeling curious and elated. All of us stuck around in our drop-off point, talking about the experience, asking questions, and wondering what it all meant. We were connected by this intimate experience, which meant something to us, at least for the last three hours. This experience still lingers in my mind, as I often wonder about the many ways it made each of us feel "seen" and "heard." An experience like this wouldn't have been possible in a room full of 200 people.

In all of these more intimate experiences, audiences forego crowds, queues, and the disappointing possibility of not being able to go on the more popular attractions. How many times have we gone to a theme park and didn't get a chance to go on the ride that we really wanted to go on? It's very frustrating, especially when we've already invested in the time and money to bring our entire family or group of friends to a day of fun.

More and more, audiences are willing to pay a higher ticket price to guarantee an A+, premium experience so that they can walk away feeling like they got everything they paid for. Places like *The Speakeasy* in San Francisco and the Magic Castle[71] in Los Angeles offer memberships

---

[71] http://www.magiccastle.com

and tiered pricing options for more "immersive" and "premium" experiences. Perhaps experiences will trend more towards private clubs such as Magic Castle or some of those secret dinner parties I keep hearing about from world-renowned chefs. (P.S. If you're reading this, Secret Chef, please invite me to one of your dinner parties!)

Although many of these smaller experiences were short-lived, I really hope that it sparked a curiosity in all of us to explore this realm further. I personally would love to go to more of these intimate experiences to fully immerse myself in a story world and connect with others in an authentic way. Experiences like these can add so much more depth and conversation. They can take you down rabbit holes that you never thought you'd ever explore. They can bring you into new worlds and open new doors of possibilities. I hope these experiences return in new and surprising ways, so that we can discover meaningful connections with others, even for a brief moment.

LAST BUT NOT LEAST

There's something very important that I want to talk about. This is something I believe all aspiring writers and storytellers for this industry should understand, especially those who are just starting out in their careers. It takes a lot of hard work and determination to succeed in this very demanding, but highly rewarding industry. I want to say, however, that no one can do it alone. I've had the support of many mentors, friends, and champions who pushed and challenged me even when I had not yet seen my own potential.

The person most responsible for my ability to pursue this career is none other than my loving husband of seventeen years. Without his support, I wouldn't be where I am today. When I had to work long hours, travel days and weeks on end, attend conferences and panels, he was the one that made sure our home didn't fall apart, that there was always dinner on the table, that the fridge was fully stocked, and that our son's homework was always checked and completed. I understand that many women don't have this support at home, especially many working mothers.

Our family at the exit of *Star Wars: Rise of the Resistance* in Disneyland.

I am so blessed to have a partner in life who believes in what I do and supports me every step of the way. It's not easy being a woman in the professional world, let alone in this industry, which requires a lot of time away from home. For working women and mothers in this industry juggling work, home, your personal, and social lives, I salute you. You are my heroes.

I want to mention this because we need to support each other. We need more men and women supporting working women and mothers. We working mothers are expected to be everything to everyone. Most of us don't get to stop working when we get home or turn off our laptops. We simply move on to our next job — being a wife and/or mom.

Society expects women to juggle our home lives, work lives, and social lives in near-perfect harmony. Many of us are held to a ridiculously high bar in the face of many double standards. We can no longer support this thinking if we hope to raise our girls into future thinkers and leaders. Instead, we all need to do our part to support the girls and women in our lives.

In my fourteen plus years of working in this industry, more than 90% of the creative directors I've worked with were white men over the age of 40. The other 10% were white women. I've never worked with a minority female creative director before. Plenty of the producers I've worked with have been women, some of them women of color, but why aren't there more creative leads who are minority women? This is a serious problem and the reasons are too varied and complex to summarize in this chapter.

What I do know is that this has to change. If we are in the business of creating experiences for people all over the world, we need to give women of color the opportunity to become creative leaders. Shouldn't experiences be explored from different perspectives rather than from one particular one? How can we change this predicament? How do we give women the opportunity to lead creatively without asking them to sacrifice other parts of their lives? How do we stop asking women to achieve an impossible double standard?

We all need to become more supportive and empathetic to working women (especially women of color). By hiring them to your team, by giving them the time they need to be with their family, by respecting their decisions, by hearing their opinions and concerns with sincerity, by giving them the spotlight, by supporting them, by letting them become their own kind of leader, by letting them bring their whole, authentic selves to work every day, by not asking them to check "motherhood" at the door before they show up for work every day.

My first writing mentor was a working mother who later introduced me to other writing gigs. Years later, I was hired at Imagineering by a working mother who was also a person of color. A couple years into the job, I was given a promotion by a woman of color. Together, we women, working parents, and people of color, need to support one another. When I came into a position where I could hire writers and other creatives, I made sure my hires were diverse and inclusive. Even if you don't identify yourself in any of these categories, we need you to do your part to support us. We can't build a career without your support and encouragement.

In addition to these women, I've had my fair share of male advocates over the years. I remember one creative director who hired me even after I just gave birth. I told him I was constantly breastfeeding and pumping, so he let me work from home. I remember the executive producer who kept volunteering me to make presentations on behalf of the creative team. I was initially terrified, but I told myself that if he believed in me, then I should believe in myself. Many dozens of presentations later, I never bat an eyelid when he (and others) asks me to speak on behalf of the team.

On top of being a working mother, I'm Asian-American, relatively "young," and an immigrant. Every day, I represent all of these groups in my workplace. Often times, I'm the only woman, person of color, mother, or immigrant in the room. I represent story in all of my projects, but I also represent so much more. There have been many instances in workplace meetings and situations where I had to speak up and stand up for myself or other people who fall under these other categories. I also had to speak up and stand up for other people who were *not* represented in the room. Other people of color, the LGBTQ community, younger generations, older generations, the list goes on and on.

As a storyteller, you hold power in your words. Not only in your written word, but also in the spoken word. The words that you choose to communicate matter. The words you choose to represent a group of people matter. There have been so many times when I've been put in difficult and uncomfortable situations where I had to listen to my gut and speak up.

What you don't say matters just as much as what you do say. At the end of the day, be proud of who you are and what you represent. Don't fear standing up for yourself or any other underrepresented group. You would hope that others would do the same for you one day.

ACKNOWLEDGMENTS

This book would not have been possible without the support and advice of Geraldine Overton, Ken Lee, and of course, Michael Wiese himself, who told me over the phone that they had been "waiting a long time to do a book like this." Thank you for believing in my work and giving me the platform to share my knowledge and experience with the next generation of storytellers.

Thank you to the following people for sharing wonderful images of their experiences:

BRC Imagination Arts: Bob Rogers
Lost Spirits Distillery: Joanne Haruta
Meow Wolf: Didi Bethurum, Brian Loo, Isabel Zermani, Candyce Handley, Gus Ortega, and Jena Braziel
Museum of Jurassic Technology: Willa Sacharow
Scout Productions: Jarrett Lantz
Sleep No More at The McKittrick Hotel: Stephanie Geyer
Spyscape: Lisa Paul, Francis Jago
teamLab Inc.: Michaela Kane and Sakurako Naka
The Speakeasy: John Hill

At Walt Disney Imagineering, there are so many people that helped to shape my career as an Imagineer. Thank you Shelby Jiggetts-Tivony and Sarah Farmer-Earll for trusting your gut, hiring me, and guiding me in my early days as a Show Writer. Thank you to Mark LaVine and Nancy Seruto for all of your encouragement and support.

Thank you to Joe Rohde and Dave Durham for giving me the opportunity to share your stories and learnings.

An enormous thank you to Jon Georges and Chris Beatty for always making me feel like an important part of the *Star Wars: Galaxy's Edge* team. From the very beginning, both of you gave me the agency and creative ownership that I needed to push the project to new heights.

Thank you to Scott Trowbridge who saw me as a true creative partner and entrusted me with the story of *Star Wars: Galaxy's Edge*. Thank you for reading the early manuscript of this book, always listening to me, and inspiring me to shoot for the stars. Terima kasih.

This book would not have been possible without the dedicated effort of the Disney team who helped to review the book and supported my pursuits outside of the company. A huge thank you to Debra Kohls, John Ward, Juliana Grisales, and Wendy Lefkon for supporting me in publishing this book.

Thank you to my sister, Caroline Tran, who has been my biggest supporter and confidante through the ups and downs of my life. For all the times you had to endure my crazy stories, pranks, and antics, thank you for always being there, laughing at my jokes, and for enjoying all of my nutty ways. As you always say, our childhood together was "training" for me to one day make up stories and entertain the world. Thanks for being my very first audience member.

Finally, I want to thank my husband of seventeen years, Foster, who has been with me every step of the way. He has been a true partner in every sense of the word. He made sure our lives didn't fall apart when I was busily working. He was the one who encouraged me to reapply to the University of Southern California MFA in Screenwriting program when I was rejected the first time I applied. He was the one who supported me through stressful, soul-crushing jobs before I found work as a writer. He was the one who made me believe that I could dedicate my life to living creatively. He is my rock. And finally, to my son, Bryce, who reminds me to play, enjoy the moment, make time for cuddles, and laugh every day. I love you both so much.

ABOUT THE AUTHOR

Born in Indonesia and raised in Singapore, Margaret received her Master of Fine Arts degree in Screenwriting from the University of Southern California School of Cinematic Arts. Her career spans television, film, digital media, games, brand storytelling, location-based entertainment, and immersive experiences. She has worked as a Story Lead, Story Consultant, and Writer for multiple projects around the world, including *Star Wars: Galaxy's Edge, Star Wars: Launch Bay, Hyperspace Mountain, Star Wars: Galactic Starcruiser, Avengers Campus, Guardians of the Galaxy: Cosmic Rewind,* National Geographic HQ, NASA Kennedy Space Center Visitor Complex's *Journey to Mars: Explorers Wanted,* Heineken Experience, Story Garden by AMOREPACIFIC, and the Information and Communications Pavilion (Expo 2010 Shanghai). She was the writer for five projects that won Themed Entertainment Association (THEA) Awards. She has appeared in the Disney+ series *Behind the Attraction,* the Freeform television special *Star Wars: Galaxy's Edge — Adventure Awaits,* and the online educational program *Imagineering in a Box.* She has been invited to speak at prestigious conferences and universities including SXSW, *Star Wars* Celebration, D23, IAAPA Expo, the Immersive Experience Institute, FMX Conference, the University of Southern California, and Johns Hopkins University. Her work has been featured around the world in *The New York Times*, *Good Morning America*, *The Los Angeles Times*, *Entertainment Weekly*, *Wired* magazine, and the official site for *Star Wars*. She was a Disney Imagineer from 2013–2021. *Immersive Storytelling for Real and Imagined Worlds—A Writer's Guide* is her first book.

She lives in Burbank, California with her husband and son, and is always looking for her next adventure in immersive storytelling.

RECOMMENDED READING LIST FOR STORYTELLERS

(IN ALPHABETICAL ORDER BY TITLE)

- *Aristotle's Poetics for Screenwriters: Storytelling Secrets From the Greatest Mind in Western Civilization* by Michael Tierno
- *Bird by Bird: Some Instructions on Writing and Life* by Anne Lamott
- *Cassandra Speaks: When Women Are the Storytellers, the Human Story Changes* by Elizabeth Lesser
- *Caste: The Origins of Our Discontents* by Isabel Wilkerson
- *Dream It! Do It!: My Half-Century Creating Disney's Magic Kingdoms* by Marty Sklar
- *Interior Chinatown* by Charles Yu
- *Minor Feelings: An Asian American Reckoning* by Cathy Park Hong
- *On Writing* by Stephen King
- *One Little Spark!: Mickey's Ten Commandments and The Road to Imagineering* by Marty Sklar
- *Save the Cat* by Blake Snyder
- *Screenplay* by Syd Field
- *Story* by Robert McKee
- *The Art of Star Wars: Galaxy's Edge* by Amy Ratcliffe
- *The Hero with a Thousand Faces* by Joseph Campbell
- *The Power of Myth* by Joseph Campbell

S.T.O.R.Y.

THE FIRST FIVE QUESTIONS

S — Share: Why share this story with the world?

T — Theme: What's the theme of the experience?

O — One-of-a-Kind: How can I make this experience unique?

R — Reflect: Why am I the best person to tell this story?

Y — Yearn: What will visitors yearn to experience? What is their wish fulfillment?

IMMERSIVE STORYTELLING QUESTIONS

(ISQ WHEEL)

WHY
- Why share this story with the world?

WHO
- Who is your audience?
- Who are the characters in your story?

WHAT
- What is the transformation you want to create in your audience?
- What is your theme?
- What is the wish fulfillment of your story?
- What are the mood and tone of your experience?
- What is the role of your audience?
- What are the rules of engagement?
- What are the emotional anchors of your experience?
- What are the comparables?

HOW
- How will your audience feel?
- How will your audience experience your story?

WHERE
- Where is the authenticity in your story?
- Where is your story set?

WHEN
- When does your story take place?

WORLDBUILDING QUESTIONNAIRE

1) Location

Is your place on Earth? In our solar system? In a fictional universe? Where exactly is it in the universe? Does it have other celestial bodies around it? If so, what? Does the location of the place support a greater significance to the story? If not, can it? What does the planet look like? What's the climate and geography? What are the natural resources?

2) History

What's your world's timeline? What are some of the major events that have shaped this place? Was there a singular event that changed the course of the people's everyday lives? How did it affect the people? What were their reactions and responses? Who were the people that lived here 100,000 years ago? 1,000 years ago? 100 years ago? 10 years ago? What was the status quo before the event and how did life change after it?

3) People and Population

What's the makeup of the population? Are there different species, races, and ethnicities? Are there different gender types? Age groups?

4) Political and Social Organization

Is there a government? Rules of politics? What's the social hierarchy? Who's on top and who's at the bottom? Are there sectors/kingdoms/countries/ cities/towns? Who's in charge? Were they always in charge? What's their livelihood? Where do they live? How do they live? Alone? In communities? What's their idea of "family" or "community?"

5) Values, Beliefs, Culture and Customs

What are their values and beliefs? Do they have religions or believe in gods? Who are these gods? What's the culture here? What are the customs? Do they have a unique language or manner of speaking? How do they greet each other? Do they have unique gestures? What's their view of the world? What do they eat? How do they eat? What do they do for fun? What are examples of their arts and culture? How do they dress? What are their mannerisms?

6) Rules of the World

Are the rules of the world based on real world laws of physics? Is there magic? If so, what kind of magic and how is it used? Who has magic? Is it desired or feared? Is there a hierarchy for people with magic? Is there a calendar? Is time similar to the real world or is there a different measure of time? Does time work in the same way? If not, how is it different?

INDEX OF LOCATIONS

Galleria dell'Accademia (Florence, Italy)

George Washington's Mount Vernon (Washington, D.C.)

Guggenheim (Bilbao, Spain)

Haunted Mansion (Disneyland, Anaheim, California)

Hearst Castle (San Simeon, California)

Hoover Dam (Nevada)

House of Sampoerna (Surabaya, Indonesia)

Infinity Mirrored Room — The Souls of Millions of Light Years Away (2013) by Yayoi Kusama

Journey to Mars: Explorers Wanted, Kennedy Space Center Visitor Complex (Merritt Island, Florida)

King Tut— Treasures of the Golden Pharaoh

Lost Spirits Distillery (Los Angeles, California; Las Vegas, Nevada)

Louvre Museum (Paris, France)

Luray Caverns (Luray, Virginia)

Mad Tea Party (Disneyland, Anaheim, California)

Magic Castle (Los Angeles, California)

Meow Wolf's *Convergence Station* (Denver, Colorado)

Meow Wolf's *House of Eternal Return* (Santa Fe, New Mexico)

Meow Wolf's *Omega Mart* (Las Vegas, Nevada)

Musee Marmottan Monet (Paris, France)

Museum of Ice Cream (New York City; San Francisco, California)

Museum of Jurassic Technology (Los Angeles, California)

Museum of Modern Art (New York City)

National Museum of African American History and Culture (Washington, D.C.)

National Museum of Natural History (Washington, D.C.)

Natural History Museum (London, United Kingdom)

The Thorne Miniature Rooms, The Art Institute of
Chicago (Chicago, Illinois)
The VOID
The Willows
The Wizarding World of Harry Potter (California
and Florida)
Tivoli Gardens (Copenhagen, Denmark)
TRON Lightcycle Power Run (Shanghai Disneyland, China)
Two Bit Circus (Los Angeles, California)
Underwood Family Farms (Moorpark, California)
Vatican Museums (Rome, Italy)
Winchester Mystery House (San Jose, California)
with all my love for the tulips, I pray forever (2011) —
Yayoi Kusama
Xcaret Park (Playa del Carmen, Mexico)

THE WRITER'S JOURNEY
MYTHIC STRUCTURE FOR WRITERS

25TH ANNIVERSARY EDITION

CHRISTOPHER VOGLER

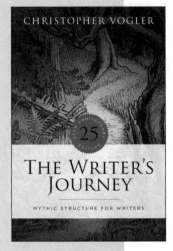

Originally an influential memo Vogler wrote for Walt Disney Animation executives regarding *The Lion King*, The Writer's Journey details a twelve-stage, myth-inspired method that has galvanized Hollywood's treatment of cinematic storytelling. A format that once seldom deviated beyond a traditional three-act blueprint, Vogler's comprehensive theory of story structure and character development has met with universal acclaim, and is detailed herein using examples from myths, fairy tales, and classic movies. This book has changed the face of screenwriting worldwide over the last 25 years, and continues to do so.

"This book is like having the smartest person in the story meeting come home with you and whisper what to do in your ear as you write a screenplay. Insight for insight, step for step, Chris Vogler takes us through the process of connecting theme to story and making a script come alive."
   —Lynda Obst, producer, How to Lose a Guy in 10 Days, Sleepless in Seattle, One Fine Day, Contact; Author, Hello, He Lied

"The Writer's Journey is an insightful and even inspirational guide to the craft of storytelling. An approach to structure that is fresh and contemporary, while respecting our roots in mythology."
   —Charles Russell, writer, director, producer, Dreamscape, The Mask, Eraser

"The Writer's Journey should be on anyone's bookshelf who cares about the art of storytelling at the movies. Not just some theoretical tome filled with development clichés of the day, this book offers sound and practical advice on how to construct a story that works."
   —David Friendly, producer, Little Miss Sunshine, Daylight, Courage Under Fire, Out to Sea, My Girl

CHRISTOPHER VOGLER made documentary films as an Air Force officer before studying film production at the University of Southern California, where he encountered the ideas of mythologist Joseph Campbell and observed how they influenced the story design of 1977's *Star Wars*. He worked as a story consultant in the development departments of 20th Century Fox, Walt Disney Pictures and Animation, and Paramount Pictures, and wrote an influential memo on Campbell's Hero's Journey concept that led to his involvement in Disney's *Aladdin*, *The Lion King*, and *Hercules*. After the publication of *The Writer's Journey*, he developed stories for many productions, including Disney's remake of *101 Dalmatians*, Fox's *Fight Club*, *Courage Under Fire*, *Volcano*, and *The Thin Red Line*.

$29.95 · 400 PAGES · ISBN: 9781615933150

© MICHELE MONTEZ

MICHAEL WIESE PRODUCTIONS

IN A DARK TIME, a light bringer came along, leading the curious and the frustrated to clarity and empowerment. It took the well-guarded secrets out of the hands of the few and made them available to all. It spread a spirit of openness and creative freedom, and built a storehouse of knowledge dedicated to the betterment of the arts.

The essence of Michael Wiese Productions (MWP) is empowering people who have the burning desire to express themselves creatively. We help them realize their dreams by putting the tools in their hands. We demystify the sometimes secretive worlds of screenwriting, directing, acting, producing, film financing, and other media crafts.

By doing so, we hope to bring forth a realization of 'conscious media,' which we define as being positively charged, emphasizing hope, and affirming positive values like trust, cooperation, self-empowerment, freedom, and love. Grounded in the deep roots of myth, it aims to be healing both for those who make the art and those who encounter it. It hopes to be transformative for people, opening doors to new possibilities and pulling back veils to reveal hidden worlds.

MWP has built a storehouse of knowledge unequaled in the world, for no other publisher has so many titles on the media arts. Please visit www.mwp.com, where you will find many free resources and a 25% discount on our books. Sign up and become part of the wider creative community!

MICHAEL WIESE, Co-Publisher
GERALDINE OVERTON, Co-Publisher

INDEPENDENT FILMMAKERS
SCREENWRITERS
MEDIA PROFESSIONALS

MICHAEL WIESE PRODUCTIONS
GIVES YOU
INSTANT ACCESS
TO THE BEST BOOKS
AND INSTRUCTORS
IN THE WORLD

FOR THE LATEST UPDATES
AND DISCOUNTS,
CONNECT WITH US ON
WWW.MWP.COM

JOIN US
ON FACEBOOK

FOLLOW US
ON TWITTER

VIEW US
ON YOUTUBE